Scrooge
The Musical

Book, Music and Lyrics by
Leslie Bricusse

Based on Charles Dickens'
A Christmas Carol

A SAMUEL FRENCH ACTING EDITION

SAMUEL FRENCH

FOUNDED 1830

New York Hollywood London Toronto

SAMUELFRENCH.COM

CAUTION: Professionals and amateurs are hereby warned that *SCROOGE - THE MUSICAL*, being fully protected under the copyright laws of the United States of America, the British Commonwealth, including Canada, and the other countries of the Copyright Union, is subject to a licensing fee, and anyone presenting the play without the consent of the owners or their authorized agents will be liable to the penalties by law provided.

Amateurs wishing to arrange for the production of *SCROOGE - THE MUSICAL* must make application to SAMUEL FRENCH, INC., at 45 West 25th Street, New York, NY 10010-2751, giving the following particulars:

(1) The name of the town and theatre or hall in which the proposed production will be presented.

(2) The maximum seating capacity of the theatre or hall.

(3) Scale of ticket prices; and

(4) The number of performances intended and the dates thereof.

Upon receipt of these particulars SAMUEL FRENCH, INC., will quote the amateur terms and availability.

Stock licensing fee and availability quoted on application to SAMUEL FRENCH, INC., at 45 West 25th Street, New York, NY 10010-2751.

For all other rights than those stipulated above, apply to Samuel French, Inc.

An orchestration consisting of **Vocal/Conductor's Score, Bass, Horn, Trombone, Trumpet I & II, Percussion, Keyboard I, II & III and 30 Vocal Chorus Books** will be loaned two months prior to the production ONLY on receipt of the royalty quoted for all performances, the rental fee and a refundable deposit. The deposit will be refunded on the safe return to SAMUEL FRENCH, INC. of all materials loaned for the production.

ISBN 978-0-573-62997-6   Printed in U.S.A.   #21029

**IMPORTANT BILLING AND CREDIT
REQUIREMENTS**

All producers of *SCROOGE - THE MUSICAL must* give credit to the Author of the Play in all programs distributed in connection with performances of the Play, and in all instances in which the title of the Play appears for the purposes of advertising, publicizing or otherwise exploiting the Play and/or a production. The name of the Author *must* appear on a separate line on which no other name appears, immediately following the title and *must* appear in size of type not less than fifty percent of the size of the title type.

Billing *must* be substantially as follows:

(NAME OF PRODUCER)

Presents

SCROOGE

Book, Music and Lyrics by

LESLIE BRICUSSE

SCROOGE — THE MUSICAL

This revised version presented by Bill Kenwright at the London Palladium on 8th November 2005 with the following cast:

Ebenezer Scrooge	Tommy Steele
Bob Cratchit	Glyn Kerslake
Harry/Young Ebenezer	Tom Solomon
Bess	Claire Parrish
Wine Merchant/Phantom/	John McManus
Dick Wilkins	
Jocelyn Jollygoode/Phantom	Richard Tate
Hugo Hearty/Mr Fezziwig	Gareth Jones
Bissett the Butcher/Phantom/	Richard Tate
Ghost of Christmas Yet to Come	
Mrs Dilber/Mrs Fezziwig	Janine Roebuck
Miss Dilber/Mary	Gemma Baird
Beggar Woman/Mrs Pringle	Emma Tapley
Punch and Judy Man/Phantom/Topper	Andrew Wright
Mr Pringle/Phantom	Martin Neely
Tom Jenkins/School Teacher	Alex Gaumond
Chestnut Seller	Joanna Fell
Jacob Marley	Barry Howard
Phantom/Sweep	Gabriel Vick
Ghost of Christmas Past	Gemma Page
Isabel/Helen	Abigail Jaye
Ghost of Christmas Present	James Head
Mrs Ethel Cratchit	Susan Humphris
Shellfish Seller	Tara Mcdonald

Nickleby Team

Tiny Tim	Laurence Belcher
Kathy Cratchit	Zizi Strallen
Peter Cratchit	Jack Haynes
Belinda Cratchit	Jody Powell
Martha Cratchit	Grace Evangelos

Sasi Strallen Spencer Fagan Jack Stark
Lucinda Francis Daniel Stark Sean Grosvenor
Georgia Walton Thyrza Abrahams Melanie Barker
Kacey Canning Dayle Hodge

Pickwick Team

Tiny Tim	Thomas Robinson
Kathy Cratchit	Kimberley Green
Peter Cratchit	Oliver Golding
Belinda Cratchit	Deanna Lashbrook
Martha Cratchit	Annabelle Green

Olivia Burley-Knox Sydney Farrington
Freddie Anthony Melissa Oden Will Brann
Dominic Welch Florence Hannon Lily Higgins
Kristi Holloway Emma Kevin Sam Duckett

Copperfield Team

Tiny Tim	Daniel Barber/Liam Buckland
Kathy Cratchit	Louisa Taylor
Peter Cratchit	Jack Sparkes
Belinda Cratchit	Amy Wilkinson
Martha Cratchit	Rebecca Bennett

Hayley Wheeler Callum Sparkes
Dominic Grainger Alice Stoner Ezekiel Martin
Joe Carling Louisa Harper Darcy Mills
Georgia Carling Rebecca Peters Alex Grainger

Director BobTomson
Décor Paul Farnsworth
Lighting Nick Richings
Sound Mick Potter
Choreography Lisa Kent
Illusions Paul Kieve
Musical Director Stuart Pedlar

SCROOGE-THE MUSICAL

First presented by Graham Mulvein in association with
D & J Arlon, Stage and Screen Music and the Alexandra
Theatre, Birmingham, on 9th November, 1992 at the
Alexandra Theatre, Birmingham, with the following
cast:

Ebenezer Scrooge	Anthony Newley
Bob Cratchit	Tom Watt
Nephew	George Asprey
Kathy Cratchit	Tanya Cooke,
	Tara Brennan
Tiny Tim	Thomas Edwards,
	Jerome Wallington
Bess	Sally Mates
Wine Merchant	Ian Caddick
Hugo Harty	David Oakley
Jocelyn Jollygoode	Harry Dickman
Butcher	John Clay
Mrs Dilber	Nanette Ryder
Miss Dilber	Lorinda King
Beggar Woman	Elaine George
Young Beggar Girls	Amy Pearson
	Maxine Loughran
Urchins	Sharon Buchanan, Simone Barnes,
	Paul Liburd, James Brown,
	John Wesley Lenegan, Ian Salter,
	Natalie Horton, Leonie Prentice,
	Thomas Wilkins, Ciaran Brennan
Punch and Judy Man	Stuart Cross
Tom Jenkins	James Head
Chestnut Seller	Johanne Murdock
Jacob Marley	Jon Pertwee
Phantom 1	Harry Dickman
Phantom 2	Stuart Cross
Phantom 3	Ian Caddick
Phantom 4	John Clay
The Ghost of Christmas Past	Julie Teal
School Teacher	James Head

Jenny	Elizabeth Eaton,
	Lara Acott
Young Ebby	Darien Smith,
	Charles Dower
Fezziwig	Dudley Owen
Young Scrooge	Richard Shelton
Dick Wilkins	Mark Channon
Mrs Fezziwig	Susannah Bray
Isabel	Catharine Duncan
The Ghost of Christmas Present	David Alder
Jack	Scan Kingsley
Prince	Thomas Paton
Raggedy Anne	Jennie Dale
Mrs Ethel Cratchit	Angie Smith
Peter Cratchit	Jonathan Kitchens,
	Lewis Nelson
Martha Cratchit	Ashley Goddard,
	Ashley Kingsbury
Belinda Cratchit	Charlotte Clark,
	Hayley Griffiths
Helen	Catharine Duncan
Topper	Paul Thornley
Mary	Sophie Caton
The Ghost of Christmas Yet-to-Come	Martin Hibbert
Boy with Sled	Nigel Cole,
	John McGivern
Mrs Pringle	Suzanne Rigden

Directed and choreographed by Tudor Davies
Production Musical Director Stuart Pedlar
Designed by Paul Farnsworth

SCROOGE—THE MUSICAL

Subsequently presented by Apollo Leisure (UK) Ltd,
Barry Clayman Concerts Ltd and James M Nederlander,
in association with Stage and Screen Music Inc., on 12th
November, 1996 at the Dominion Theatre, London,
with the following cast:

Ebenezer Scrooge	Anthony Newley
Bob Cratchit	Tom Watt
Harry	Richard Shelton
Kathy Cratchit	Julia Harrison-Jones
Tiny Tim	John Faal,
	Jamie Meyer
Bess	Susannah Bray
Wine Merchant	Mark Channon
Mr Pringle, the Toy Shop owner	James Head
Jocelyn Jollygoode	Steve Elias
Hugo Harty	Dudley Owen
Bissett, the butcher	Martin Hibbert
Mrs Dilber	Judith Street
Miss Dilber	Sophie Caton
Beggar Woman	Suzanne Rigden
Urchins	Summer Vaingcourt-Strallen,
	Jessica Playfoot, Ross Goddard,
	Nigel Cole, Adam Stiles,
	Stephanie Seager, Gemma Castleman,
	Natalie Kelly, John McGivern,
	Ian Middleton, Thomas Gray
Punch and Judy Man	Paul Thornley
Tom Jenkins	Sean Kingsley
Chestnut Seller	Amelia Jane
Jacob Marley	Stephen Earle
Phantom 1	Martin Hibbert
Phantom 2	Thomas Paton
Phantom 3	Mark Channon
Phantom 4	Paul Thornley
The Ghost of Christmas Past	Felicity Soper
School Teacher	Sean Kingsley

Jenny	Kate Butler,
	Rachel-Louise Humpage
Ebby	Lawrence O'Rourke,
	Glen Bate
Fezziwig	David Oakley
Young Scrooge	George Asprey
Dick Wilkins	Neil Couperthwaite
Mrs Fezziwig	Sally Mates
Isabel	Joanne Heywood
The Ghost of Christmas Present	Stratford Johns
Jack-in-the-Box	John Tobias
Mrs Cratchit	Sarah Hay
Peter Cratchit	James Edge,
	Jonathan Woolf
Martha Cratchit	Elizabeth McTernan,
	Sarah Jane Jeffery
Belinda Cratchit	Donna Bosworth,
	Tracey Buller
Helen	Joanne Heywood
Topper	Stuart Cross
Mary	Lorinda King
Party Guest	Cheryl Jane King
Older Posh Girls	Louisa Smythe,
	Donna Watkins,
	Hayley-Jayne Adams,
	Gemma Marie Humpage
The Ghost of Christmas Yet-to-Come	John Clay
Boy with Sled	Thomas Wilkins
Mr Pringle, the toy shop owner	Ian Caddick
Mrs Pringle, his assistant	Elaine George

Directed by Bob Tomson
Choreographed by Anthony Lapsley
Production Musical Director Stuart Pedlar
Designed by Paul Farnsworth

CHARACTERS

Ebenezer Scrooge
Bob Cratchit
Nephew
Kathy Cratchit
Tiny Tim
Bess
Wine Merchant
Mr Carstairs
Hugo Harty
Jocelyn Jollygoode
Bissett, the butcher
Mrs Dilber
Miss Dilber
Beggar Woman
Urchins
Punch and Judy Man
Tom Jenkins
Jacob Marley
Phantoms
The Ghost of Christmas Past
School Teacher
Jen
Ebby
Fezziwig
Young Scrooge
Dick Wilkins
Mrs Fezziwig
Isabel
The Ghost of Christmas Present
Jack-in-the-Box
Mrs Cratchit
Peter Cratchit
Martha Cratchit
Belinda
Helen
Topper
Mary

Party Guests
The Ghost of Christmas Yet-to-Come
Boy with Sled
Mr Pringle, the toy shop owner
Mrs Pringle, his assistant
Tradespersons, Children, Barrel-rollers, Apprentice Boys, Bakery Girls, Winery Boys, etc.

SYNOPSIS OF SCENES

ACT I

SCENE 1	A London Street—Cheapside
SCENE 2	Scrooge's office
SCENE 3	A London street—Cheapside
SCENE 4	The exterior of Scrooge's lodgings
SCENE 5	Scrooge's hallway
SCENE 6	Scrooge's bedroom
SCENE 7	A school room
SCENE 8	Fezziwig's warehouse
SCENE 9	Ebenezer's office
SCENE 10	Scrooge's bedroom
SCENE 11	Scrooge's bedroom
SCENE 12	A London street—Cheapside

ACT II

SCENE 1	A London street—Cheapside
SCENE 2	The Cratchits' house
SCENE 3	Scrooge's Nephew's sitting-room
SCENE 4	Scrooge's bedroom
SCENE 5	The street outside Scrooge's office
SCENE 6	The Cratchits' house
SCENE 7	The churchyard
SCENE 8	Scrooge's bedroom
SCENE 9	A London street—Cheapside
SCENE 10	The Cratchits' house
SCENE 11	A London street—Cheapside

MUSICAL NUMBERS

ACT I

1	**Opening**	Company
1a	Underscore	
2	**M.O.N.E.Y.**	Scrooge
3	A Christmas Carol – Underscore	
4	**Christmas Children**	Bob Cratchit, Tiny Tim, Kathy, Company
4a	**Father Christmas**	Tom Jenkins, Miss Dilber, Mrs Dilber, Bess, Bissett, Punch & Judy Man, Beggar Woman, Wine Merchant, Company
5	**I Hate People!**	Scrooge, Company
5a	Scene Change	
6	**Make The Most Of This World**	Marley, Phantoms
7	**It's Not My Fault**	Scrooge
8	**A Christmas Carol**	Staff, Children
8a	Schoolroom – Underscore	
9	**December the Twenty-Fifth**	Fezziwig, Mrs Fezziwig, Chorus
10	**Happiness**	Ebenezer, Isabel, Scrooge, Christmas Past
10a	You - You – Underscore	
11	**You - You**	Scrooge, Young Ebenezer
11a	**Love While You Can**	Christmas Past
12	**It's Not My Fault** (Reprise)	Scrooge
13	**Finale Act I**	Christmas Present, Scrooge, Company

ACT II

14 Opening of Act II

15 **The Milk of Human Kindness**   Tom Jenkins, Boozers, Quartet, Landlord

15a The Beautiful Day – Underscore

16 **The Beautiful Day**   Tiny Tim, Cratchits

16a I Like Life – Underscore

17 **The Minister's Cat**   Mary, Guests

17a December the Twenty-Fifth – Instrumental

18 **Happiness** (Reprise)   Scrooge

18a Happiness – Underscore

19 **A Better Life**   Scrooge

20 **Thank You Very Much**   Scrooge, Tom Jenkins, Company

21 **The Beautiful Day** (Reprise)   Tiny Tim (voice over), Bob Cratchit

22 **I'll Begin Again**   Scrooge

22a Christmas Children (Prelude to Finale)

23 **Finale Act II**   Company

23a **I'll Begin Again** (Reprise)   Scrooge, Off stage Chorus

24 **Curtain Calls**   Company

24a **Thank You Very Much**   Company

25 Playout

Musicals by Leslie Bricusse in the series
"Leslie Bricusse Musical Classics"
published by Samuel French Ltd

Pickwick (based on Charles Dickens' *Posthumous
Papers of the Pickwick Club*)
The Revenge of Sherlock Holmes
Scrooge (based on Charles Dickens'
A Christmas Carol)
Henry's Wives

ACT I

Scene 1

A London Street—Cheapside. Christmas Eve

Church bells chime six o'clock

No. 1: Opening

The Curtain *rises on a tableau of a Dickensian Christmas card—circa 1843—a crowd of Shoppers, Street Vendors and Children. A tumbling profusion of Christmas fare fills the street stalls and shops. The tableau comes to life*

Kathy	The first Noel, the angel did say...
Tom Jenkins	God rest you merry, gentlemen, let nothing you dismay...
Jollygoode/Harty	Good Christian men, rejoice with heart and soul and voice...
Company	O come, all ye faithful...
	Good Christian men, rejoice with heart and soul and voice...
Cratchit	Silent night, holy night, silent night...
Miss/Mrs Dilber	The first Nowell...
Jollygoode/Harty	The holly and the ivy, when they are both full grown...
Jenkins	Ding dong ding ding-a dong-a ding...

All
Sing a song of gladness and cheer,
For the time of Christmas is here!
Look around about you and see
What a world of wonder this world can be!

Sing a Christmas carol—
Sing a Christmas carol—
Sing a Christmas carol—
Like the children do!
And enjoy the beauty—

All the joy and beauty—
That a merry Christmas
Can bring to you!

The crowd mingle and wish each other a Merry Christmas

Sing a song of gladness and cheer,
For the time of Christmas is here!
Look around about you and see
What a world of wonder
This world can be!

Sing a Christmas carol—
Sing a Christmas carol—
Sing a Christmas carol—
Like the children do!

And enjoy the beauty—
All the joy and beauty—
That a merry Christmas
Can bring to you!

The people begin to disperse, revealing:

SCENE 2

Scrooge's office

Scrooge's clerk, Bob Cratchit, is asleep whilst writing at a tall desk in the corner of the dingy room

The front door crashes open and we see the figure of Scrooge

Scrooge CRATCHIT!!

Bob jolts awake scattering his papers. Scrooge marches in, taking off his outdoor garments

I hate Christmas! Humbug! ... People? I hate people. Yuletide-loving, second-rate people... It's all a load of humbug I tell you...

We hear Urchins singing just outside Scrooge's front door

Urchins (*in strident cacophony*) 'Ark the 'erald hayngels si-hing
                        Glory to the new-born king!
                        Peace on 'erf—an' mercy mi-hild——
1st Urchin (*aggressively*) Jesus Christ, that little child!

They continue to sing as Scrooge mutters angrily to himself

Scrooge Infernal horrible caterwauling! Don't they know I'm trying to
  run a business here?

There is a pounding on the door and Cratchit looks up fleetingly

  Get on with yer work, Cratchit! Bah! Humbug! Insolent young ruffians,
  coming here with their Christmas nonsense ... bah!

*The singing gets louder and Scrooge grabs his walking stick and stomps
towards the door*

  Hell-fire and damnation! Why can't they leave a man in peace! (*He pulls
  open the door*)

*A charming, elegant and smiling young man stands before him, his
nephew, Harry. The Urchins run off, laughing*

Scrooge (*scowling*) Oh, it's you.
Nephew Uncle Ebenezer, I cannot tell you what a joy it is to see your
  happy smiling face. And how are you, Bob?
Bob Cratchit Very well, thank you, sir.

*Scrooge scowls his disgust and turns back to his desk. The Nephew follows
him jauntily into the office and closes the door. He gives Cratchit a friendly
nod and a wink and follows Scrooge to his desk*

Nephew A merry Christmas, Uncle Ebenezer! God save you!
Scrooge God save me from Christmas! It's a lot of humbug! (*He swiftly and
  expertly counts up a handful of gold sovereigns, drops them into the money
  box and slams it shut to underline the sentiment. He picks up the money box
  and carries it over to the safe*)

*The Nephew perches himself in carefree fashion on the corner of Scrooge's
desk*

Nephew Christmas a humbug? Come now, I'm sure you don't mean that!
Scrooge And I'm sure I do mean that! Merry Christmas, indeed! What
  reason have *you* to be merry? You're poor enough!

Nephew And what reason have you to be miserable? You're rich enough!

Scrooge There's no such thing as rich enough! Only poor enough! (*He rams the money box deep into the safe and slams and locks the door with much clanging of metal*)

Nephew Don't be so dismal, Uncle Ebenezer!

Scrooge What else can I be, when I live in a world of fools babbling "Merry Christmas" at one another? What's Christmas but a time for finding yourself a year older and not a day richer? (*He thrusts his face menacingly at his nephew*) If I could work my will, Nephew, every idiot who goes about with "Merry Christmas" on his lips should be boiled with his own pudding and buried with a stake of holly through his heart!

Nephew God forbid, Uncle!

Scrooge You keep Christmas in your way, and let me keep it in mine!

Nephew But you don't keep it!

Scrooge Then let me alone! And be good enough not to bother me, sir, during business hours. And get off me ledger—you'll ruin me binding!

The Nephew gets up off the desk and looks at his fob watch. Scrooge picks up the heavy ledger, examines the binding for possible damage and, with a reproachful glare at his Nephew, carries it across to a dusty bookcase and locks it away with a key from his watch-chain

Nephew Seven o'clock on Christmas Eve? That's not business hours! That's drudgery for the sake of it, and an insult to all men of goodwill!

Bob Cratchit (*muttering under his breath*) Hear, hear!

Nephew Thank you, Bob Cratchit!

Scrooge Another word from you, Cratchit, and you'll celebrate Christmas among the great unemployed.

Bob Cratchit Yes, sir. I'm sorry, Mr Scrooge.

The Nephew pulls a crusty face at his uncle, converting it into an instant smile as Scrooge turns to him

Scrooge You're quite a powerful speaker, sir. I wonder you don't go into politics—you're fool enough!

The Nephew roars with laughter. Scrooge returns to his work

Nephew Come now, don't be angry! Dine with my wife and me tomorrow!

Scrooge There's another thing! As though you hadn't got enough problems, you went and got married! Now why in God's name did you do that?

Nephew Because I fell in love with the lady.

Scrooge (*opening another ledger with a growl*) Love! If there's one thing in the world more nauseating than "Merry Christmas", it's a happy marriage with some love-sick female! Good-afternoon, sir!
Nephew My offer stands. You are always welcome, Uncle—just like Christmas itself!
Scrooge I said good-afternoon!

No. 1a: starts (underscore)

Nephew I want nothing from you. I ask nothing of you. Why can we not be friends?
Scrooge Good-afternoon!
Nephew Merry Christmas, Uncle. And you too, Bob Cratchit! And your family!
Bob Cratchit (*with a smile*) Thank you, sir. And to your good lady!

The Nephew exits, then reappears in a second, popping his head round the door

Nephew Oh, and Uncle!
Scrooge Hmmm?
Nephew A happy New Year!
Scrooge (*furiously*) Good-afternoon, sir!

The Nephew exits, grinning

Bob Cratchit, considerably cheered up, warms his hands on the candle on his desk. The chimes of a nearby church are heard

Bob Cratchit Excuse me, sir, but it's—er—seven o'clock, sir.

Scrooge looks at his watch

Scrooge (*grudgingly*) Correct, Cratchit.
Bob Cratchit I don't wish to be impertinent, Mr Scrooge, but will it be too much trouble if I have my wages, sir?

Scrooge growls his disapproval and reluctantly stops work and takes out his purse, carefully counting out fifteen shillings as they talk. He counts it three times—twice in his own hand, and finally into Cratchit's hand

Scrooge The trouble with you, Cratchit, is that all you think about is money! You'll be wanting the whole of Christmas Day off tomorrow, I suppose?
Bob Cratchit If it's convenient, sir.

Scrooge It is not convenient, sir. And it is not fair. And yet if I stopped your wages for it you'd think yourself ill-used, no doubt. Aren't I ill-used, when I pay a day's wages for no work?

Bob Cratchit Well, it *is* Christmas Day, Mr Scrooge. And it *is* only once a year, sir.

Scrooge A poor excuse for picking a man's pocket every twenty-fifth of December! I don't pay good money for you to be forever on holiday!

Bob Cratchit I appreciate your kindness, Mr Scrooge.

Scrooge That's my weakness—I'm a martyr to me own generosity! I give you one Christmas Day off and you expect' em all! Very well, take the day. But be here all the earlier next morning!

Bob Cratchit Oh, I will, sir. Yes, sir. Thank you, sir. And a merry Christmas, Mr Scrooge.

Scrooge (*thundering*) A merry what!?

Bob Cratchit I mean, I beg your pardon, sir. No offence, sir.

Bob scuttles quickly out of the door

Scrooge immediately hurries across to blow out the meagre candle still burning on Cratchit's desk

Scrooge (*grumbling to himself*) There's another one. Fifteen shillings a week, a wife and five children, and still talks about a merry Christmas. Belong in a lunatic asylum, the lot of 'em... Humbug! (*He obsessively starts to lock, bolt, bar and chain every door, drawer, cupboard and window of his establishment He takes every possible precaution, even locking the sole remaining piece of coal in the coal-scuttle in his safe*)

No. 2: M.O.N.E.Y.

(*Singing*) Everywhere you look—everywhere you turn—
Someone's after every single penny that you earn!
Everyone's a thief!—that is my belief!
Anyone who says they're not is sure to come to grief.
I seek but I shall never find
A deeper peace of mind—
'Cos I'm convinced that everyone
Is out to rob me blind!
Accumulating money is the quest of all mankind!
And God forbid that Ebenezer Scrooge be left behind!

There is only one God up in heaven on high,

And I'll worship his name till the day that I die!
He alone rules the world from a bright golden sky,
And our saviour's name is M.O.N.E.Y.!

There is only one power man can never deny.
There is only one force that we dare not defy.
Nothing else on this earth do we all glorify
As our one true master M.O.N.E. Y.

Other forms of worship,
They come and they go
And most of them fade in a flash
'Cos most of them are mere cant and trash!
The one faith to believe in, where there's no
   misconceivin'
No nonsense and no grievin' is C.A.S.H. cash!
Rough and ready, strong and steady cash!

There is only one cause I can just justify
To make life here in Cheapside at least worth a try,
And since I've no desire to devour humble pie,
I devote my life to M.O.N.E.Y.

I shall spend my whole life gazing at,
Admiring and appraising, that amazing man-made
   miracle
There's nothing it can't buy!
 And that's the reason why I'll save it till I die!
M.O.N.E.Y.!

The music segues into **No. 3: A Christmas Carol** *underscore*

SCENE 3

A London street—Cheapside

Outside in the busy street, a lame boy, Tiny Tim, stands with his sister Kathy, gazing in awe at the display window of a large toy shop. The centre-piece of the window is a magnificent model carousel, revolving to the melody of A Christmas Carol. *Behind the carousel is a glittering Christmas tree, groaning beneath the weight of every conceivable Christmas toy and treat hanging from its branches*

8

We see Bob Cratchit emerging from the bakery stall with a small parcel in his hands

Bob Cratchit Fourpence for a Christmas pudding—it's scandalous!
Baker Woman Sorry.

Cratchit joins his two children, clutching their meagre shopping, as they stare into the toy shop's window

Bob Cratchit Well, Kathy, my love, which one do you like best?
Kathy I like that doll in the corner.
Tiny Tim I like all of 'em!
Bob Cratchit Good boy! And why not one in particular?
Tiny Tim Well, you said I can't have none of 'em, so I might as well like 'em all!
Bob Cratchit Tiny Tim, you are a philosopher and a gentleman, and I've still got twelve shillings left in me pocket...
Kathy/Tiny Tim (*impressed*) Twelve shillings!
Bob Cratchit Twelve shillings, which says the Cratchit family will have as good a Christmas as the Lord Mayor of London 'imself.

He kisses the little boy's face and lifts him up on to his shoulder. As they move away from the window, the music starts under

Tiny Tim (*in awe*) Twelve shillings!
Kathy I do like that doll in the corner!

Christmas Children (No. 4) starts (underscore)

The Cratchits move on to a laden fruit stall

Bess With your lot to feed, Bob Cratchit, I'd say the apples at six a penny are the best bet. (*She puts the apples in Cratchit's basket*)
Bob Cratchit (*handing her the money*) True, Bess, true.
Kathy (*to Tim*) I'd rather have that dolly in the corner.
Tiny Tim I'd rather have the oranges.

They move on to the wine store. The Wine Merchant is serving a wealthy customer

Wine Merchant (*placing three bottles into a carpet bag*) Your change, Mr Carstairs. Eighteen-forty is the best vintage in twenty years!
Mr Carstairs At two shillings a bottle, it should be! A happy Christmas to you!

Wine Merchant And a happy Christmas to you, sir! (*He spots Bob Cratchit and fills an empty bottle from a stone jar*) This'll make the finest quality punch, Mr C, and only tuppence a pint.

Bob Cratchit takes the bottle and pays the twopence

Bob Cratchit Oh, thank you, sir. (*He smiles at Tim and Kathy*) Christmas punch—a Cratchit speciality.

Tiny Tim pulls Kathy back towards the toy shop window

Tiny Tim Let's look at that toy theatre again, Kathy. I bet it costs about a million pounds!
Kathy The price tag says two pounds and ten shillings.
Tiny Tim Well, that's about a million, isn't it?

No. 4: Christmas Children

Bob Cratchit Christmas children peep into Christmas windows—
See a world as pretty as a dream.
Christmas trees and toys—
Christmas hopes and joys—
Christmas puddings rich with Christmas cream.

As they move along the street full of Christmas shoppers, the laden-down luxury of well-to-do shoppers contrasts with the meagre purchases of the Cratchits. A well-dressed mother and her two daughters emerge from the toy shop with a mountain of beautifully wrapped parcels, carried by their footman and coach driver

	Christmas presents shine in the Christmas windows
	Christmas boxes tied with pretty bows.
Kathy	Wonder what's inside?
Tiny Tim	What delights they hide?
Bob Cratchit	But till Christmas morning no-one knows.
Kathy	(*sighing*) Won't it be exciting if it snows?

Tim and Kathy gaze up at an enormous turkey hanging outside the butcher's shop

Company	I suppose that children everywhere.
	Will say a Christmas prayer...

Bob Cratchit picks up a somewhat scraggy goose and pays the butcher

Bob Cratchit   Till Santa brings their Christmas things...

(*Speaking*) There, my loves, I've brought the finest bird in the shop...
Well, the finest for one and fourpence!

Company   Christmas children live in a Christmas daydream—
                      Waiting for the magic to unfold.
Tiny Tim   Wond'rous things to eat—
Kathy   Ev'ry Christmas treat—
Bob Cratchit   Rich or not, the Christmas pot of gold
                      Hypnotizes children young and old...

Bob surveys the scene around him with deep satisfaction

Company   I suppose
                      That children everywhere
                      Will say a Christmas prayer...
Bob Cratchit   Till Santa brings their Christmas things.
Company   Christmas children hunger for Christmas morning.
                      Christmas day's a wonder to behold.
                      Young ones' dreams come true
                      Not-so-young-ones', too!
Bob Cratchit   I believe that story we've been told—
Company   Christmas is for children young and old!

Piled high with packages, the Cratchits head happily home

*Scrooge enters, scowls into the toy shop window, then spots two chortling
ladies who are full of Christmas cheer, Mrs Dilber and Miss Dilber,
owners of a knitwear stall*

Mrs Dilber (*fearfully*) Oh—it's Mr Scrooge.
Scrooge Two pounds five shillings, ladies.
Mrs Dilber Mr Scrooge, sir, we've been giving more credit than usual.
Scrooge So have I. Two pounds five shillings!
Miss Dilber As it's Christmas, sir, we've given people an extra week or two
    to pay...
Mrs Dilber Shhh...
Scrooge Aha! Then I shall give *you* an extra week to pay!
Mrs Dilber (*incredulously*) Oh, thank you, sir...
Scrooge Which will cost you a further twelve shillings!
Miss Dilber Twelve shillings!
Scrooge Unless you would prefer me to confiscate your stall and its contents
    — which is my legal right...

Mrs Dilber No, sir, we'll pay, sir.

Bissett, the Butcher, passes by, carrying a giant turkey

Scrooge Bissett!
Bissett Please, Mr Scrooge, a few more days.
Scrooge You've already had a few more days! If you can afford to stock
    turkeys like that, you can afford to pay me! You can give me two
    pounds of kidneys and I'll give you another three days.

The Butcher is resigned to the inevitable outcome

Bissett Very well, Mr Scrooge. Thank you, Mr Scrooge, two pounds
    of kidneys.
Scrooge Wrap 'em up and I'll take them home!

*Scrooge makes his way to the Punch and Judy show, where a crowd of
children are cheering Punch. Scrooge pushes past the children into the tiny
Punch and Judy tent*

Judy Oh, Mr Punch, I've lost my little baby. Where is she?
Scrooge He's here, Miller. And you owe me two pounds seven and six.
Punch and Judy Man Not now, Mr Scrooge—*please!* I'm performing!

Their two heads appear, filling in the tiny stage

Scrooge (*surveying the audience of children*) Pity it doesn't pay you
    better! Where's my money?
Punch and Judy Man Tomorrow, for sure, Mr Scrooge... it's my best
    day of the year!
Scrooge Tomorrow it will be two pounds ten ... or your puppets belong
    to me!

The Children boo him. Scrooge scowls at them

Punch and Judy Man All right, Mr Scrooge. Two pounds ten!

The Children boo again. Judy points at the departing Scrooge

Judy (*to Punch*) That man's even meaner than you are.

*Punch hits Judy with his stick. The Children laugh. The Punch and Judy Man
continues his show. Scrooge spies another debtor, Pringle the Toyshop
Owner. A Beggar Woman and her child proffer a begging bowl*

Beggar Woman (*carrying a baby*) Merry Christmas, sir! A penny for
the little one?

Scrooge Madam, the financial burdens of my life are already intolerable:
pray don't add to them by asking me to pay for the upkeep and education
of your entire family! (*Calling*) Pringle!

Pringle Mr Scrooge, sir!

Scrooge A word.

Father Christmas (No. 4a) starts (underscore)

> *Pringle reluctantly opens the door of his shop and the two men enter in to
> conduct their business in private*

Tom Jenkins (*sarcastically*) There 'e goes— Father Christmas himself!

*As Tom sings, other Tradespersons, victims of Scrooge's "Christmas Spirit"
gather round the soup trolley to swap opinions. The number has a dark
and threatening feel*

(*Singing*)	Father Christmas—Father Christmas—
	'E's the meanest man
	In the 'ole wide world!
	In the 'ole wide world'
	You can feel it!
Miss Dilber	'E's a miser!
Mrs Dilber	'E's a skinflint!
Tom Jenkins	'E's a stingy lout—
	Leave yer stocking out
	For yer Christmas gift—
Bess	An' 'e'll steal it!

They all roar with laughter

Tom Jenkins	It's a shame—
	'E's a villain!
Bissett	What a game
	For a villain to play...

Punch and Judy Man On Christmas Day!

Company   After Christmas,
                       Father Christmas
                       Will be just as mean
                       As 'e's ever been...

Tom Jenkins   An' I'm 'ere to say
                       We all should send Father Christmas...
                       On 'is merry Christmas way!

Another group of dissatisfied Traders have collected. The song builds into a full company production number, in which the people of Cheapside join Tom Jenkins and the Urchins in venting their spleen on the villainous and miserly Scrooge

Company   On Christmas Day!
Beggar Woman   'E's a rascal!
Wine Merchant   'E's a bandit!
Tom Jenkins   'E's a mean old bean
                       As we all 'ave seen
                       An' I'm 'ere to say
                       We should all send Father Christmas
                       On 'is merry Christmas——

They are cut off in midflow by Scrooge who enters from the toy shop, gleefully scribbling a sizeable addition to his accounts. He is followed by a grim-faced Mr Pringle

Scrooge peruses the toy shop window with scorn

Scrooge Dolls, toys, bows and arrows! Waste of money... Christmas...! Humbug!
Pringle And a merry Christmas to you, Mr Scrooge.

Scrooge consults his black book again and approaches the last stall, run by a personable young man, Tom Jenkins. The music continues quietly under

Tom Jenkins (*to a customer*) There we are, sir, thank you very much.
Wine Merchant Merry Christmas, Tom.
Tom Jenkins (*spotting Scrooge approaching*) Merry Christmas to you, sir.
Scrooge No.
Tom Jenkins Hot broth, Mr Scrooge... a small token of Christmas esteem, with the compliments of Tom Jenkins!

Scrooge No.

Tom Jenkins (*hastily*) And there'll be a free can of broth every night throughout the coming year, sir...

Scrooge No.

Tom Jenkins In gratitude for your infinite kindness in giving me another two weeks to pay!

Scrooge One week.

Tom Jenkins Ten days.

Scrooge One week.

Tom Jenkins One week.

Scrooge And put a lid on that stuff—I'll take it home.

Tom Jenkins does as he is bid

Scrooge, muttering and grumbling, is suddenly aware of the two portly gentlemen, Jollygoode and Harty, standing behind him. He scowls suspiciously as they bow to him, smiling

Jollygoode Good-evening, sir...

Harty Allow us to introduce ourselves...

Jollygoode Jocelyn Jollygoode...

Harty And Hugo Harty... Have we the pleasure of addressing Mr Scrooge or Mr Marley?

Scrooge Mr Marley has been dead these seven years; seven years this very night.

There is an ominous rumble of thunder. The company begin to pack up and make their way homewards

Jollygoode We have no doubt his liberality is well represented by his surviving partner.

Scrooge (*his eyes narrowing at the offensive word*) Liberality?

Harty Mr Scrooge, sir, at this festive season of the year, it is more than usually desirable that we should make some slight provision for the poor and the destitute.

Scrooge Excellent. Then I suggest you do so.

Jollygoode You miss our point, sir. The poor suffer greatly at the present time. Many thousands are in want of common necessaries.

Scrooge Are there no prisons?

Harty Indeed there are, sir. That's one thing there's no shortage of!

Scrooge And the workhouses? Are they still in operation?

Jollygoode They are, sir, and I wish I could say they were not.

Scrooge The treadmill and the Poor Law are in full vigour, I trust.

Jollygoode Both very busy, sir.

Scrooge I am very glad to hear it! For a moment I was afraid something had occurred to stop them in their useful purpose!

Harty A few of us are endeavouring to raise a fund to buy the poor some meat and drink, and means of warmth.

Jollygoode We choose this time because it is a time when want is keenly felt, and abundance rejoices. What may we put you down for, sir?

Scrooge Nothing, sir.

Harty You wish to be anonymous?

Scrooge I wish to be left alone, sir—that is what I wish. I don't make myself merry at Christmas, and I cannot afford to make idle people merry. I have been forced to support the establishments I have mentioned through taxation ... and those who are badly off must go there!

Jollygoode Many would rather die than go there!

Scrooge If they would rather die, then they had better do it, and decrease the surplus population! Yes, gentlemen ... decrease the surplus population!

Harty and Jollygoode drift away leaving Scrooge satisfied with his victory

No. 5: I Hate People

(*Singing*) Scavengers and sycophants and flatterers and fools!
Pharisees and parasites and hypocrites and ghouls!
Calculating swindlers! Prevaricating frauds!
Perpetrating goodness as they roam the earth in hordes!
Feeding on their fellow men, reaping rich rewards!
Contaminating everything they see!
Corrupting honest men—
Like me!

I hate people!—I hate females!
Women are a maddening species
Watch one closely and you'll see she's
Out to make you see what she sees.
I hate women
Picked at random
I can't stand them.

Fools who have no money spend it—
Get in debt and try to end it!
Beg me on their knees befriend them—
Knowing I have cash to lend them!

Soft-hearted me! Hard-working me!
Clean-living, thrifty and kind as can be!
Situations like this are of "interest" to me! Interest...

Scrooge   I hate Christmas

                                    Company Father Christmas!
                         I hate people!

                                            Father Christmas!

Yuletide-loving, second-rate people
That is why I treat them like vermin
I delight in seeing them squirmin'
Many fools have tried to determine
What can his motive be?

What's the reason?

                                            He's a miser!

I hate Christmas —

                                            He's a skinflint!

I hate people —
Women, children —
'Specially nasty, smelly children!
Well, I'll tell you   He's a rascal!
What's the reason   He's a bandit!
                                 He's a mean old man!

It's because they all
Hate me!

Scrooge whirls his stick as the crowd scatter in all directions

   Humbug!

A great crack of thunder as the Lights reveal the front door of:

SCENE 4

The exterior of Scrooge's lodgings

Scrooge arrives at his own front door and fumbles with his keys

Shivering with cold, Scrooge stands in the silent gloom of the doorway. A large gargoyle-head door-knocker glares at him inscrutably. Scrooge finds the right key and places it in the lock As he looks up, the gargoyle-head in the door-knocker becomes a human face. Suffused with a ghastly light, it stares at Scrooge and breathes his name in a deep mournful voice

Marley's face Scroo-o-o-o-ge...
Scrooge (*transfixed with terror*) Marley? Jacob Marley?
Marley's face Scroo-o-o-o-ge!

The ghastly light fades. Scrooge shakes his head and goes inside

Scrooge Bah... Humbug!

SCENE 5

Scrooge's hallway

Scrooge picks up a candle-holder from a table near the doorway and nervously lights the candle. The flickering flame casts macabre and eerie shadows on the walls. The wind gathers strength. Scrooge freezes again, candle and soup-can poised, as the bizarre sound reaches his ears. The wind howls around him, and a ghostly voice seems to call through it

Scrooge Humbug! It's voices in the mind! All voices in the mind!
Marley's voice Scroo-oo-oo-ooge...
Scrooge (*gulping*) It's voices in the wind. Voices in the wind!
Marley's voice Scroo-o-ooge!
Scrooge It's not possible! Not possible!

Scrooge stands transfixed with terror as the volume of sound accumulates. Then he runs for his sitting-room and slams the door, his own footsteps augmenting and multiplying in sound until the entire building is reverberating with the deafening echoes of a thousand running footsteps. Scrooge locks, bolts and bars his door, then leans against it, breathing heavily, listening to the retreating sound waves

SCENE 6

Scrooge's bedroom

The room contains Scrooge's bed, bedside table with an alarm clock, a straightbacked chair, and a hob with a spoon and a bowl ready next to it. An old wing-backed armchair stands near the fireplace. A miserable fire burns

*Scrooge carries the soup-can and the candle across to the fireplace. He
places the soup-can on the hob. A mournful wind moans in the chimney, and
Scrooge remains ill-at-ease. He takes off his coat and hangs it and his high
hat in a cupboard*

*He pulls the armchair close to the hearth, pours the gruel from Tom Jenkins's
soup-can into the bowl and settles back into his chair to enjoy it*

*As he raises the first spoonful to his lips, his hand starts to shake uncontrollably,
slopping the gruel back into the bowl. The wind moans mournfully in the
chimney and seems to echo his name. Smoke suddenly billows out*

Wind Scroo-oo-o-ooge!
Scrooge (*resolutely*) It's humbug still! I'll not believe it!
Wind Scroo-oo-o-ooge!

*Scrooge stares wild-eyed at a bell beside the fireplace in front of him as it
slowly starts to swing. At first it makes scarcely a sound. Then it gathers
strength, swinging wildly back and forth. The sound of other bells fills the
night with unaccustomed sounds. Scrooge puts down his bowl of gruel and
clasps his hands over his ears as the bells reach a deafening crescendo*

*Suddenly there is total silence. Scrooge's eyes dart suspiciously from side to
side. He takes his hands from his ears and listens intently. A deep hollow
clanking sound and heavy footsteps are audible outside his door. Scrooge
rushes to the door and puts his ear to it. Reverberating echoes of dragging
chains and creaking doors and dismal wailing and muffled footsteps are
intermingled and orchestrated into a mounting nightmare of sound. Scrooge
double-locks the door and hurries back to his chair, looking round the edge
of it in unconscionable distress. He takes a cash box hidden in the fireplace
and puts it under his pillow. He then sits in the chair again*

*His eyes widen in horror as first one bolt of the door, and then another, slide
themselves open. The key in the door turns and unlocks itself once, twice,
without the aid of a human hand*

*Scrooge jumps to his feet again, grabs a poker from the fireplace to defend
himself if necessary, then hurries towards the door as though to re-lock it. He
stops short as he suddenly hears an increasing sound of rushing, howling
wind assailing the door from outside. The door shakes and rattles under, the
strain. Scrooge emits a great wail of fear as the door suddenly flies open and
a great rush of icy air blows across the room*

And framed in the doorway he sees ... the fearful apparition of the ghost of Jacob Marley

Marley (*wailing*) Ebenezer Scroo-o-ooge!

The door slams shut

Whimpering with fear, Scrooge edges warily forward to the door, opens it and looks out into the blackness beyond. There is no-one there. The door is open 180 degrees

Scrooge Hallo? Hallo? (*He closes the door*) It's all humbug!

Standing behind the door, inside the room, is Marley's ghost

Marley Ebenezer Scrooge!

Scrooge whirls round with a cry of terror

Marley is swathed in a great chain made up of cash-boxes, ledgers, keys, padlocks, deeds and heavy purses. Scrooge contemplates in horror this fearful reincarnation of his former partner

Scrooge H-how now! What do you want with me?
Marley Much!
Scrooge Who are you?
Marley Better to ask me who I was.
Scrooge Who were you, then?
Marley In life I was your partner, Jacob Marley.
Scrooge Jacob? Can you sit down?
Marley Of course I can sit down.
Scrooge Please do so, then.

Marley sits, with much clanking and evident relief. Scrooge averts his eyes

Marley You don't believe in me, do you?
Scrooge No, I don't.
Marley Why do you doubt what you see?
Scrooge Because I've had a slight stomach disorder. It has undoubtedly affected my vision. You're an hallucination, probably brought on by an undigested bit of beef, or a blob of mustard. Yes, that's what you are—you're a blob of mustard!
Marley I tell you, Scrooge, there's more of the grave than of gravy about me!

Scrooge You do not exist, Jacob Marley! Humbug, I tell you—humbug!

Marley Humbug—eh? (*He pulls his chin away from his mouth*) Now do you believe in me?

Scrooge Absolutely! I thank you for your visit and for your good counsel, and now, sir, (*he opens the door*) I bid you a fond farewell.

Marley closes the door with a hand gesture

But why do you walk the earth? And why do you come to me?

Marley I am doomed to wander through the world and witness what I cannot share, but might have shared on earth, and turned to happiness. (*Again he utters a desolate cry and shakes his chain, as though overwhelmed with remorse*)

Scrooge trembles

Scrooge And why are you fettered by that great chain?

Marley I wear the chain that I forged during my life on earth. I made it link by link and yard by yard, and now I can never be rid of it. Any more than you will ever be rid of yours.

Scrooge (*trembling*) M-m-mine?

Marley Imagine the weight and length of the mighty chain you are making for yourself. It was as heavy and as long as this seven Christmasses ago! You have laboured at it mightily ever since! It's a terrible ponderous chain you are making, Scrooge.

Scrooge Jacob! Old Jacob Marley! Speak comfort to me! (*He instinctively looks about his person for the chain and is relieved to find it not there*)

Marley I have none to give. Very little is permitted to me. I cannot rest, I cannot stay, I cannot linger anywhere... When I lived, my spirit, like yours, never walked beyond the narrow limits of our counting-house.

Scrooge But you were always a good man of business, Jacob.

Marley Business? Mankind is our business, Ebenezer. But how seldom do we attend to it! I know this because I have sat invisible at your elbow many and many a day in your office.

Scrooge (*shivering at the thought*) My office? Watching me?

Marley Hear me, my time is almost gone. I am here tonight to warn you. It is your only hope.

Before Scrooge can object, Marley throws a loop of his chain over his erstwhile partner's neck, and the door and windows slowly open allowing strange lights and mist to enter

Scrooge (*terrified*) No, Jacob! No-o-o-o!

The air around them is filled with moaning Phantoms, ghostly, ghastly figures like Marley, horrific to behold, green and grey and white and yellow, haunted half rotted skeletal figures, their faces and shapes grotesquely distorted by the eternal horrors that haunt them, and fettered like Marley with the appropriate symbols of their selfish lives

Scrooge, shaking with fear, covers his eyes and whimpers like a frightened child. Marley pays him no heed. The Phantoms join him in a macabre song of foreboding

No. 7: Make the Most of This World

Marley (*with deep gloom*) See the phantoms filling the room around you!
    They astound you,
    I can tell—
    These inhabitants of hell.
    Poor wretches
    Whom the hand of heaven ignores.
    Beware! Beware! Beware!
    Lest their dreadful fate
    Be yours!

Phantoms moan

    Make the most of this world—
    The next world is worse!
    If you think life is miserable now—
    But the life to come is better somehow—
    You had better put
    All your thinking in reverse—
    And make the most of this world—
    For the next world
    Is far, far worse!

Marley and Make the most of this life—
Phantoms The next life's a curse!
    The man who kicks the present aside—
    In a quest for things life doesn't provide—
    Had better know now this theory is perverse—
    And make the most of this life—
Marley   For the next life
    Is far, far worse!

    Let's talk about heaven a minute—

Men dream of it from birth.
Heaven—you idiot!
You're in it on earth!

Marley and Phantoms	So make the most of living—
	'Cos dying is worse!
	At times you'll say life isn't worthwhile—
	But there's more to life
	Than travelling in style!
Marley	It's better to walk
	Than ride inside a hearse!
Marley and Phantoms	So make the most of this world—
	Embrace the universe!
Marley	For I guarantee
	The next world
	Is far, far worse!

The Phantoms fade

The door and windows close. At the end of the song, Scrooge drops emotionally exhausted on to the bed and closes his eyes for a few seconds. Suddenly his eyes open wide. He listens. All is quiet

Scrooge (*smiling*) It was a dream!

Marley's ghost is sitting in the armchair, facing him

Marley It was not a dream, Scrooge.
Scrooge (*leaping to his feet*) For pity's sake, Marley, leave me in peace!
Marley It was for pity's sake that I came here. Pity for you! I leave you now with just the tiniest chance of escaping my fate!

Scrooge looks slightly cheerful for the first time since he met the apparition

Scrooge You were always a good friend to me, Jacob.
Marley You will be visited by three spirits.
Scrooge I—I think I'd rather not.
Marley The first will appear tonight when the bell tolls one.
Scrooge Couldn't I take 'em all at once, and get it over with?
Marley The second at two o'clock, and the third when the bell tolls three. Listen to them, and learn from them.

In the distance, midnight strikes

I must go now, for I am doomed to wander through the world in everlasting repentance.

Scrooge Marley, wait!

Marley Look to see me no more, and, for your own sake, remember what has passed between us! Farewell, Ebenezer Scrooge! Pray for me!

Marley raises his arm high above his head and rises into the air and disappears from view, back up into the spirit world

Scrooge looks around the empty room. He lights a candle. Both he and the candle are shaking as he carries it nervously across the room towards his curtained four-poster bed. The music starts under as Scrooge undresses for bed, and he sings the song as he goes through the motions of changing into a long nightgown and a pom-pommed nightcap. He keeps on the heavy full-length winter underwear that is revealed when he removes his outer clothes. Bedsocks and slippers complete his night regalia. He then winds and sets the alarm clock on the table beside his bed

No. 7: It's Not My Fault!

Scrooge
Damn you, Marley!
This is hardly
How you treat
A trusted friend!

Curse you, Jacob!
Can't you make
A better dream—
And change the end?

I suppose this gives you joy!
You no doubt think it's funny, eh?
Knowing you, it's all a ploy
For you to steal my money, eh?

(*Speaking: hysterically*) Well, you shan't have it! You shan't have it!

You can't just come back from the dead
An' dump your guilt on me!
Begone!—you and your phantoms, sir!
And leave the living be!

Especially me!
Especially me!

It's not my fault
You are dead and I'm alive!
It's not my fault
You succumbed and I survive!

Is it my fault
Fate has fashioned things this way?
Is it my fault
That tomorrow's Christmas day?
These things happen anyway!
You can't blame me
If the sun decides to shine!
So don't blame me
That the life I live is mine!

(*Modestly*) *A* life of quiet sobriety—
Of which I'm justly proud!
A credit to society—
Who shuns the vulgar crowd!
Who uses wisely all the gifts
With which he's been endowed!

(*Smugly*) A good man—a philanthropist—
Who's truly worth his salt!
No, it's not—my—fault!

Three ghosts...? Three humbugs!

It's you who left our counting house—
To find a bigger vault
To find a bigger vault!
No, it's not—my—fault!

He kicks off his slippers and clambers into the four-poster bed, drawing the bed-curtains closed for warmth and protection. He opens the front curtains again almost immediately as a nearby church clock strikes the full chimes of one o 'clock with a deep melancholy boom

(*Counting each quarter of the chimes*) A quarter past! ... Half past! ... A quarter to! The hour! ... and nothing else?

A blinding light fills the room as the Ghost of Christmas Past appears. She materializes miraculously, out of the high-backed chair in which Scrooge was sitting

Scrooge sits bolt upright in bed with a startled cry, staring at the unexpected figure that confronts him. It is a pretty young woman

Who are you?

Christmas Past I am the Spirit whose coming was foretold to you.

Scrooge You don't ... look like a ghost.

Christmas Past Thank you.

Scrooge May I enquire more precisely who or what you are?

Christmas Past I am the Ghost of Christmas Past.

Scrooge Long past?

Christmas Past No. Your past. I am the ghost of all the loved ones you have lost.

Voices (*off*) The loved ones you have lost.

Scrooge And what business brings you here?

Christmas Past Your welfare.

Scrooge To be woken by a ghost at one o'clock in the morning is hardly conducive to my welfare.

Christmas Past Your redemption, then.

Scrooge gasps with fear and recoils as the Ghost reaches out and touches his arm

Come—walk with me.

Scrooge protests as the vice-like grip of the Ghost removes him gently but firmly from his bed

Scrooge Madam! It is a bitter cold night outside, and as you see, I am in my night apparel...

Christmas Past No matter.

Scrooge Where are we going?

Christmas Past We are going to look at your childhood.

Scrooge No!!

Scene 7

A school-room

The room is sparsely furnished with a row of school benches. There is a pile of labelled suitcases nearby

A happy group of Schoolchildren are celebrating that uniquely wonderful end-of-term, breaking-up-for-the-school-holidays feeling. The Children are conducted by their Teacher

No. 8: A Christmas Carol

Children   Sing a song of gladness and cheer—
and Staff   For the time of Christmas is here!
                       Look around about you and see
                       What a world of wonder this world can be!

                       And enjoy the beauty
                       All the joy and beauty
                       That a merry Christmas
                       Can bring to you!

Teacher Merry Christmas, boys.
Children (*chattering in unison*) Merry Christmas, Mr Bleak, sir!

The children cheer and disperse

Scrooge, his hands clasped in delight, stands with the Ghost of Christmas Past, re-living a moment of childhood

Scrooge This is my old school. I knew these people...

The children exit as though in a dream, their voices fading back into the past

Christmas Past Look. The school is not quite empty, is it? A solitary boy, neglected by his father, is left there still.
Voice (*off*) Neglected by his father.

On the now empty stage, a lonely boy, Ebenezer, sits on a hard chair, reading, half curled up to protect himself from the cold. Scrooge sees his forgotten self as he used to be, and blows his nose

Scrooge Poor little fellow! It's me! It's poor little me! (*To the Ghost*) But I could never join in those Christmas things... I wish...

Schoolroom (No. 8a) starts (underscore)

Christmas Past What is it?
Scrooge Nothing. Nothing.
Christmas Past What do you wish?
Scrooge There were some boys singing a Christmas carol at my door last night. I should like to have given them something, that's all. (*He looks sadly at his former self*)

The Ghost of Christmas Past smiles at him

Christmas Past   But this Christmas was special.

Jen, Scrooge's sister, runs in and embraces the little boy, kissing him fondly

Jen   Ebby?Ebby?

Scrooge   Oh, look, it's my little sister. (*Calling out and waving*) Jenny! ... Jen! Why doesn't she wave back?

Christmas Past   She cannot see or hear you. These are but the shadows of things that have been.

Voices   (*off*) Shadow of things that have been.

Jen   Ebby, dear, dear brother, I have come to bring you home!

Ebenezer   Home to Father? No.

Jen   Father has paid off all his debts and is so much kinder than he used to be so I was not afraid to ask him if you might come home. He sent me in a coach to bring you. And you're going to be a man, Ebby, and never come back here again. We'll be together all Christmas long and have the merriest time in all the world. Collect your things.

Ebenezer picks up his few meagre possessions, and follows his sister off

Christmas Past   (*watching them*) Always a delicate creature, whom a breath might have withered. But she had a large heart.

Scrooge   So she had, I'll not deny it.

Christmas Past   She died a young woman, and had, I believe, children.

Scrooge   She had one child.

Christmas Past   Ah yes ... your nephew! Harry...

Nephew   (*off*) I ask nothing of you. Why can we not be friends?

Scrooge   (*a bit uneasy*) Yes... My nephew...

Christmas Past   (*looking into the distance, pointing*)   Now there's a Christmas you really enjoyed!

Mr Fezziwig   (*off*) Christmas you really enjoyed.

Scene 8

Fezziwig's warehouse

December the 25th (No. 9) starts (underscore)

Two Young Men wheel in a desk so tall that the head of the plump, jolly, middle-aged gentleman sitting at it is near the ceiling. He looks at his fob watch, roars with laughter and rubs his hands with delight. The Young Men start to re-arrange the benches

Scrooge (*amazed*) It's old Fezziwig! I was his apprentice!
Fezziwig (*raising his desk bell*) Ebenezer! Dick!

> *Scrooge's former self, now a young man in his twenties, comes forward. He is played by the same actor who plays Scrooge's nephew. They must not be too identical, but bear a strong family resemblance. He is accompanied by his fellow apprentice, Dick*

> Yo-ho, Ebenezer! Yo-ho, Dick! No more work today, my boys! Hilli-ho! Chirrup! It's Christmas Eve, Dick! Christmas, Ebenezer! Now come along, clear everything away before a man can say Jack Robinson and make some room here, before Mrs Fezziwig and me daughters arrive with the punch bowl.

Ebenezer and Dick leap into action

Other Apprentice Boys and Men swarm about

Scrooge nudges the Ghost

Scrooge My word, I am a good-looking chap! And that other fellow! Dick Wilkins, his name was. Best friend I ever had.

Fezziwig scutters up and down as the office and warehouse are transformed in an instant from a place of business to a party setting. Balloons and multicoloured twists of ribbon are festooned around the warehouse signs, which read "Fezziwig's Fine Wines and Ales", and "Mrs Fezziwig's Famous Foodstuffs—Cakes and Pastries a Speciality"

> *The equally jolly Mrs Fezziwig approaches at the head of a Christmas party procession bearing all manner of delicious burdens. She erupts into the room. She has brought the entire party with her—food, drink, decorations and music, together with the Bakery Girls and Winery Boys as her party guests, laden with packages. Everybody carries something. A very pretty girl, Isabel, walks smilingly alongside Mrs Fezziwig, carrying a beautifully decorated, multi-tiered Christmas cake*

Ebenezer (*nudging Dick Wilkins; indicating the girl*) That's Isabel, old Fezziwig's daughter. Isn't she wonderful? (*He sighs dreamily*)
Dick Wilkins (*grinning at him*) You've got about as much chance of getting close to her as I have...

Isabel trips. The multi-tiered cake teeters alarmingly. Both are about to fall. In a flash Ebenezer is beside her. He puts his arm around her waist to steady her, and with the other he steadies the cake. Everybody cheers

Fezziwig Well done, Ebenezer!

Isabel dazzles him with a grateful and flirtatious smile

Isabel   Thank you, Ebenezer.
Dick Wilkins (*nudging Ebenezer*) You *are* a fast worker. Now you can have your cake and eat it, too!

The merriment redoubles as the embarrassed Ebenezer grins and shrugs awkwardly and rejoins Dick Wilkins. Fezziwig greets his wife with a smacking kiss and holds up his hand for silence

Fezziwig Mrs Fezziwig, my darling Isabel, my dear friends, thanks to our heroic Ebenezer there will now be happiness and contentment in this room, the like of which none of us has ever seen before!
Mrs Fezziwig (*beaming*) Consumption of fewer than six cakes and three beakers of punch per person will be penalized by instant dismissal from the party!

Everybody cheers

Fezziwig Splendid! Begin!

The Fiddler starts playing, and to a roar of approval from the Company, old Fezziwig launches into the opening song and dance of the party with his lady

No. 9: December the Twenty-fifth (*continues*)

Fezziwig	Of all the days
	In all the year
	That I'm familiar with—
	There's only one
	That's really fun—
Chorus	December the twenty-fifth!
Fezziwig	Correct!
Mrs Fezziwig	Ask anyone called Robinson
	Or Brown or Jones or Smith
	Their favourite day

	And they will say—
Chorus	December the twenty-fifth!
Mrs Fezziwig	Correct!

Chorus	December the twenty-fifth, me dears.
	December the twenty-fifth.
	The dearest day in all the year—
	December the twenty-fifth!
Both	Correct!

Scrooge, lost in reverie, taps his toe in time to the music

Christmas Past (*to Scrooge*) And why didn't you join in?
Scrooge (*embarrassed and crusty about it*) Because I couldn't dance.

| **Chorus** | December the twenty-fifth! |

Fezziwig	At times we're glad
	To see the back
	Of all our kin and kith—
Mrs Fezziwig	But there's a date
	We celebrate—
Chorus	December the twenty-fifth!
Fezziwig	Correct!

Mrs Fezziwig	At times our friends
	May seem to be
	Devoid of wit and pith—
Fezziwig	But all of us
	Are humorous—
Chorus	December the twenty-fifth!
Mrs Fezziwig	Correct!

Chorus	December the twenty-fifth, me dears.
	December the twenty-fifth.
	The dearest day in all the year—
	December the twenty-fifth!

*The Ghost of Christmas Past points across the room to the lonely figure of
the young Ebenezer watching the dance*

| | December the twenty-fifth, me dears. |
| | December the twenty-fifth. |

The dearest day in all the year—
December the twenty-fifth!

Mrs Fezziwig If there's a day in history
That's more than any myth—
Beyond a doubt
One day stands out—
Chorus December the twenty-fifth!
Mrs Fezziwig Correct!

Mr Fezziwig I don't hear any arguments,
Mr and Mrs So may I say forthwith
Fezziwig I wish that every day could be
December the twenty-fifth!
Chorus Correct!

Scrooge punches the Ghost's arm enthusiastically. The Ghost winces. The dance continues against the dialogue. The Fiddler controls the operation from atop Fezziwig's lofty desk, and the warehouse is now a whirl of dancing figures

Fezziwig and December the twenty-fifth, me dears.
Company December the twenty-fifth.
The dearest day in all the year—
December the twenty-fifth, me dears.
December the twenty-fifth, me dears.
December the twenty-fifth, me dears.
December the twenty-fifth!
Correct!

Scrooge (*speaking*) What a marvellous man!
Christmas Past He has merely spent a few pounds of your mortal money—three or four, perhaps. What is that to be deserving of so much praise?
Scrooge (*looking at her disapprovingly*) You don't understand. He had the power to render us happy or unhappy—to make our work a pleasure or a burden. It's nothing to do with money! ... nothing to do with money!

He sees the Ghost looking at him knowingly

Happiness (No. 10) starts (undercore)

Christmas Past What's the matter?
Scrooge Thinking again.

Christmas Past Of what?
Scrooge Bob Cratchit.
Christmas Past Who's Bob Cratchit?
Bob Cratchit (*off*) It's seven o'clock. Can I have my wages, please, sir?
Scrooge (*hastily*) No-one. (*He dismisses the matter and returns his attention to the festivities around him*)

The music of December the Twenty-fifth has now dissolved into Happiness, and the dancers waltz gently around the floor to its easy rhythm. Isabel is watching the young Ebenezer. Scrooge catches his breath. He cannot take his eyes from her

Isabel walks over to Ebenezer, inviting him to dance. Ebenezer's shyness borders on panic, but with a warm and reassuring smile she gently coaxes him on to the floor. He is gauche and uncoordinated, but Isabel nods her encouragement

The other dancers slowly disappear from view, until Isabel and Ebenezer are dancing alone

(*Whispering*) She taught me to dance... Isabel... Ah, those were wonderful days, you know.

No. 10: Happiness

Ebenezer	They say happiness is a thing you can't see ——
	A thing you can't touch——
Isabel	I disagree.
	Happiness is standing beside me.
	I can see him. He can see me.
	Happiness is whatever you want it to be.

Scrooge (*speaking*) She adored me. I can't say I blame her.

Isabel	Happiness is a high hill.
	Will I find it? Yes, I will.
	Happiness is a tall tree.
	Can I climb it? Watch and see.
Scrooge	They say happiness is the folly of fools.
	Pity poor me—one of the fools.
Ebenezer	Happiness is smiling upon me.
	Walking my way, sharing my day.
Scrooge and Ebenezer	Happiness is whatever you want it to be.

Scrooge (*speaking*) She was so sweet and kind.
Christmas Past   Yes, she was. She still is. Adored by her family, her children, her grand-children. You missed it all, Scrooge, Why?

Isabel and	Happiness is a bright star.
Ebenezer	Are we happy?
Isabel	Yes, we are.
Isabel and	Happiness is a clear sky
Ebenezer	Give me wings and let me fly.
	Let me fly.

Ebenezer kisses Isabel's hand

Scrooge, Ebenezer (*sadly*) For happiness is whatever you want it to be.
and Isabel
Christmas Past   Yes, happiness is whatever you want it to be.

As the song ends, Ebenezer slips a ring on to Isabel's finger. Gazing lovingly into each other's eyes, they return to the slow waltz

Music segues into 10a: You – you underscore

Scrooge sniffs audibly and gazes wistfully at the Ghost of Christmas Past as the figures fade from view

Scrooge   I did love her, you know.
Christmas Past   Did you?
Scrooge   Oh, yes. I loved her.
Christmas Past   Then why did you let her go?
Isabel (*voice off*) Why did you let her go?

Scrooge smiles in sad bewilderment

Scrooge (*guiltily*) I didn't.
Christmas Past   Really?
Scrooge   She left me.
Christmas Past (*with some anguish*) Quick. My time grows short.
Scrooge   No!!

SCENE 9

Ebenezer's office

A more mature-looking Ebenezer is engrossed in work at his desk as Isabel enters, carrying a bunch of flowers

Isabel Ebenezer?
Ebenezer Yes. (*He does not look up from his work*)

Isabel picks out the fading flowers from the vase on Ebenezer's desk and replaces them with the fresh ones. Old Scrooge is right beside her, and now looks at her with a sadness greater than her own

Ebenezer is preoccupied

Isabel We have talked of marriage for quite some time. But there is still no plan for a wedding.
Ebenezer There will be a wedding when I have enough money to support such an enterprise.
Isabel When will that ever be, Ebenezer? How much is "enough"? I want to marry you, not your cash box.

Slowly Ebenezer looks up at Isabel as her words penetrate

Ebenezer I will decide when. I will know. Now I have work to do.

Isabel shakes her head. She looks sadly at the ring Ebenezer gave her

Isabel No. You have found another love to replace me—and she is much more desirable than I am.
Ebenezer I have no idea what you're talking about.

Isabel puts her hand in the open money box on the desk and lets a handful of golden sovereigns trickle through her fingers

Isabel This lady here.

Ebenezer puts his pen down and looks at the gold, and then at Isabel

Ebenezer How shall I ever understand this world? There is nothing on which it is so hard as poverty, and there is nothing it condemns with such severity as the pursuit of wealth!
Scrooge He's right! It was true then and it's true now!
Isabel All your nobler dreams, that I loved, I have seen die off, one by one, until only the desire for gain is left.
Ebenezer I am not changed towards you ... am I?
Isabel Yes, Ebenezer. You are. Your promise to me was made when you were poor, and content to be so. You were someone else then. I see that only too clearly, and so I can release you. (*She looks sadly again at the ring, then removes it from her finger and offers it to Ebenezer*)

Ebenezer does not take it

Ebenezer   Have I ever asked to be released?
Isabel   In words, no. But in a changed nature, yes. In everything that made my love of value to you, yes. If you met me today, you would not love me.
Scrooge   (*vehemently*) I would! I do!
Christmas Past   Ssssh!
Scrooge   (*sadly*) I still do...

Ebenezer remains silent. Isabel touches the pair of scales on the desk, placing the little ring on one side, and a pile of gold coins on the other. The scale moves accordingly

Ebenezer   Isabel, I find it impossible to discuss personal affairs during business hours. Now please.
Isabel   You see? If you weigh me by gain, I weigh very little. And so I am not enough for you, and I release you—with a full heart, for the love of him you once were.

Ebenezer goes to speak, but Isabel turns away

Scrooge   Say something, you fool! Say something!

Ebenezer struggles to say something

Isabel   You may have pain in this. But it will pass, and you will dismiss the recollection of it gladly, as an unprofitable dream, from which it happened well that you awoke.

Ebenezer shakes his head. Isabel kisses his cheek

Scrooge   Don't go... It's a mistake ... don't go!
Isabel   Be happy in the life you have chosen.

Isabel walks to the door and exits

Scrooge   Isabel. Isabel!
Ebenezer   Isabel...

But she has gone. Scrooge looks brokenly at Ebenezer

Scrooge   Go after her!
Ebenezer   I can't!

Ebenezer turns his back and walks away

Scrooge You fool! (*To himself*) You fool!

No. 11: You –You

Scrooge	You—you were new to me
	You—you were spring.
Ebenezer	You—you were true to me
Scrooge	You—you were everything.
Ebenezer	You—you were good for me.
Scrooge	You were my day.
Ebenezer	Did all you could for me.
Scrooge	I let you go away.
	And now I can see—
	Now you're a dream gone by.

Ebenezer and	Oh, how could there be
Scrooge	Such a fool as I?

Ebenezer returns to his desk and his work. Scrooge remains looking out after the lost Isabel

Ebenezer and	You—you were sweet to me,
Scrooge	You filled my heart,
	Life seemed complete to me—
	I thought we'd never part.

But now you are gone—
And oh, what might have been!
My life will go on—
But what will it mean?

Ebenezer picks up the ring and looks at it sadly. Scrooge looks at the same ring, which he still wears, on a string around his neck

Ebenezer	I, who must travel on,
	What hope for me?
Scrooge	Dream where my past has gone—
	Live with a memory—
Scrooge and	You, my only hope —
Ebenezer	You, my only hope —
	You—You—You...

Scrooge Spirit, remove me from this place, I can bear it no more.

Scrooge's bedroom reappears around them

Scene 10

Scrooge's bedroom

Christmas Past I have brought you home. I must leave you soon, and return
to the other side.
Scrooge No, don't go. There is so much I need to talk about.
Christmas Past Well then, why do you not love your nephew, Harry?

Scrooge looks uncomfortable

Scrooge Harry?
Christmas Past He is my son.

Scrooge, horrified, recognizes the ghost as that of his dead sister

Scrooge Your son? Jenny? ... Jen. Is that you?
Christmas Past Yes, Ebby, my dear, dear brother.

She is called back to the other side

There is so little time...
Scrooge Come back!
Christmas Past There's no coming back, Ebby ... which is why you must
never hide your love from those you cherish.
Scrooge (*lost*) Jenny...

No. 11a: Love While You Can

Christmas Past   Love while you can, all your life while you can—
Since the day time began, man's had no greater plan.
Don't be afraid to have love in your heart
Share your love with the world, it will not fall apart.
Use each magic moment well, while you are free to
    choose them,
Make each precious friendship tell, only too soon you
    lose them.

Scrooge (*speaking*) Jen—I don't want to lose you.

Christmas Past   Take my advice let love drift through your life.
                     Make a gift to your life and befriend every man.
                     My bequest to you, the best that you can do
                     Is to love while you can—
                     Love while you can.

The Ghost of Christmas Past disappears through Scrooge's mirror

Scrooge Jenny! Don't leave me again!
Christmas Past Goodbye, Ebby. My dear, dear brother. Don't forget me,
don't forget me, don't forget me...

She has gone. Scrooge turns away from the mirror in revulsion and fear.
Heartbroken and dispirited, he is alone once more in his dismal bedroom

Scrooge Then go ... but haunt me no longer!

<h2 style="text-align:center">Scene 11</h2>

Scrooge's bedroom

No. 12: It's Not My Fault! (Reprise)

Scrooge   It's not my fault
                         If I choose to live alone!
                         It's not my fault
                         If I'm happier on my own!

                         Is it my fault
                         That I lose the ones I love?
                         Is it my fault
                         Or some greater power above
                         Who enjoys destroying love?

                         You can't blame me
                         For the fickle ways of fate
                         So don't blame me
                         For the things I've come to hate

                         (*Wistfully*) There was a time I might have lived
                         A different kind of life—
                         Sweet evenings with friends and things—
                         With children ... and a wife!

> But now to even think of it
> Cuts through me like a knife!

He regains control and feigns anger

> I can't just turn life upside-down
> With one great somersault—
> No ... no ... no
> No, it's not—my...

The church bell strikes two o'clock. A strange glow of light pervades the darkened room. Scrooge mutters to himself

Two o'clock... "The second comes at two"! (*After a few seconds of paralysis and indecision he swiftly slips out from the bed curtains. He sits waiting. Calling out*) I'm ready for you, whatever you are! I'm not afraid, I'm not afraid, I'm not afraid!

The silence is overwhelming

(*Trembling; terrified*) There's nothing to be afraid of!

The room is still and silent, but the glow of light is stronger. Scrooge walks slowly across the room. A deep, disembodied voice booms eerily through the house

Christmas Present (*off*) Ebenezer Scrooge!

Immediately Scrooge is back at the foot of the bed, his hands on his palpitating heart

Come here, Scrooge! I'm waiting for you!

Scrooge obediently leaps away from the bed again. He cowers in a corner

Scrooge (*his eyes shut tight*) Is that—er—you again, Jacob Marley, m-my old friend?
Christmas Present (*off; thundering*) No, it's not!

The glow of light intensifies. Scrooge, still whimpering, shields his face as deep menacing music builds to a climax and then stops. Scrooge opens his eyes—and to what a sight

His entire bed, canopy and all, rises up into the air to reveal a cornucopian feast and a setting of breathtaking opulence and abundance. The light softens. His room has been transformed into the very vision of Christmas. Holly, mistletoe and ivy hang everywhere. Heaped on the floor are turkeys, geese, game and poultry, great joints of meat, suckling pigs, mince-pies, plum puddings, barrels of oysters, red-hot chestnuts, immense twelfth-cakes and seething bowls of punch that fill the room with steam

> *Enthroned amidst this glorious setting sits a superb and jolly Giant, wearing a magnificent deep green velvet robe bordered with ermine, and on his head a holly wreath, set with icicles that sparkle like outsize diamonds*

Scrooge Who are you?

Christmas Present I am the Spirit of Christmas Present! Look upon me! You have never seen the like of me before!

Scrooge Never.

Christmas Present And yet how many of my brothers have you rejected in your miserable lifetime?

Scrooge I have never met your brothers, sir.

Christmas Present You have never looked for them!

Scrooge How many of them are there?

Christmas Present What year is this?

Scrooge Eighteen hundred and forty-three.

Christmas Present Then I have eighteen hundred and forty-two brothers! This year it is my turn. Each year at this time, one of us visits this puny little planet to spread some happiness, and to remove as many as we can of the causes of human misery! (*He leans closer to Scrooge, his voice a menacing rumble*) Which is why I have come to see you, Ebenezer Scrooge!

Scrooge (*suspiciously*) And what do you want with me?

Christmas Present You're a funny-looking little creature! I must admit I found it hard to believe that you would be as horrible as my brothers said you'd be, but now that I look at you I can see they were understating the truth!

Scrooge (*with dignity*) Let me assure you, sir, that I am a man of the highest principles and the most generous spirit!

Christmas Present Generous spirit! You don't know the meaning of the phrase—but you are about to find out! Drink this! (*He pours some white fluid into two huge chalices and hands one to Scrooge*)

Scrooge What is it?

Christmas Present Taste it!

Cautiously Scrooge sniffs at the drink, then sips it. He pauses, then drains the chalice dry. The Ghost nods and smiles

Christmas Present   Do you like it?

Scrooge It's wonderful! I've never tasted anything like it!

Christmas Present   Of course you haven't!

Scrooge What is it?

Christmas Present   The milk of human kindness. There are more good
  things in life, Scrooge, than you can possibly imagine!

Scrooge   I'm sure there are! Can I have some more?

The Giant sings in a booming bass voice

No. 13: Finale Act I

Christmas Present   Ebenezer Scrooge,
                        The sins of man are huge.
                        A never-ending symphony
                        Of villainy and infamy,
                        Duplicity, deceit and subterfuge.
                        And no-one's worse than Ebenezer Scrooge!

                        Though a man's a handy candidate for hell,
                        I must admit
                        Life sometimes has
                        Its brighter side as well!

                        I like life! Life likes me!
                        Life and I fairly fully agree—
                        Life is fine! Life is good!
                        'Specially mine,
                        Which is just as it should be!

*He tops up Scrooge's goblet every time Scrooge takes a drink, which is
frequently*

                        I like pouring the wine,
                        And why not?
                        Life's a pleasure
                        That I deny not!

                        I like life! Here and now!
                        Life and I made a mutual vow.
                        Till I die,
                        Life and I
                        We'll both try to be better somehow!

And if life were a woman,
She would be my wife!

Scrooge   Why?
Christmas Present   Why?
Because I
Like life!

Scrooge (*speaking*) That's all very well for you! I hate life!

The Ghost roars with laughter and pours Scrooge another immense goblet of the milk of human kindness. Scrooge suddenly becomes morose and depressed. He is quite drunk

Christmas Present Nonsense, man. Why?
Scrooge Because life hates me! That's why!
Christmas Present Scrooge, you're an even bigger fool than I took you for! You've had over sixty years on this earth in your long, miserable, selfish existence, and you still don't even know how to live! Now listen to me.

(*Singing*) I like life ... (*speaking*) well, go on.
Scrooge (*singing reluctantly*) I like life...

As he sings, Christmas Present lavishes food and drink on Scrooge, who mellows visibly and gradually emerges from his gloom

Christmas Present That's better.
(*Singing*) Life likes me!
Scrooge   Life... (*he gulps*)... likes me...
Christmas Present (*speaking*) Good, good.
(*Singing*) I make life a perpetual spree!
Scrooge (*less than coherent*) Perpetual spree!
Christmas Present Eating food!
Scrooge   Drinking wine!
Christmas Present Thinking who'd
Like the privilege to dine me!
Scrooge   I like drinking
The drink I'm drinking!
Christmas Present That's better, Scrooge, and...

I like thinking
The thoughts I'm thinking!
I like songs!
I like dance!
I hear music and I'm in a trance!

Scrooge	Tra-la-la!
Christmas Present	Oom-pa-pah!
Both	Chances are
	I shall get up and prance!
Christmas Present	Where there's music and laughter,
	Happiness is rife!
Scrooge	Why?
Christmas Present	Why?
	Because I like ...

*The music builds as the Giant raises his arms to heaven in a majestic gesture
as Scrooge's bedroom dissolves*

Christmas Present   Come on, Scrooge, we're going visiting. You're in
   for a few surprises!

The music continues

Scene 12

A London Street—Cheapside. Late on Christmas Eve

*We see a church choir issuing out of church to collect charity money.
Jollygoode and Harty are with them. We see Harry and his wife delivering
gifts. Street Urchins run about*

*We see Tom Jenkins, the Dilbers, and the Beggar Woman having drinks
outside the pub "The Holly and the Ivy"*

*We see a troupe of Street Entertainers bringing a brave splash of colour and
enchantment to the street*

We see the Cratchit family staring with amazement at the scene

Children	Sing a Christmas carol
Men	Sing a Christmas carol
Sop/Alto	Sing a Christmas carol
Alto/Bass	Like the children do
Sop/Ten	Like the children do
Alto/Men	Sing a song of gladness and cheer
	Sop Sing a song, sing a song
Alto/Men	For the time of Christmas is here
	Sop Christmas is here

Alto/Men	Look around about you and see		
	Sop See——		
Alto/Men	What a world of		
All	Wonder this world can be		

Women	And enjoy the beauty	**Men**	Sing a Christmas carol
	All the joy and beauty		Sing a Christmas carol
	That a merry Christmas		Sing a Christmas carol
All	Can bring to you		

The music builds to an irresistible climax

**All (with Full
  Company
  off stage)** }   Because I—like—life!

The Ghost fills Scrooge's chalice to overflowing as he and Scrooge laugh and laugh

CURTAIN

ACT II

No. 14: Opening Act II

Scene I

The same location: Cheapside, London street. 2am on Christmas Morning

As the Choirmaster says good night to Messrs Jollygoode and Harty, a great noise is heard from inside "The Holly and the Ivy". A very merry Tom Jenkins comes from the pub, with the Dilbers, Lamplighter, Street Entertainers, Beggar Woman and Pub Landlord, Christmas Present observes

No. 15: The Milk of Human Kindness

Tom Jenkins
The milk of human kindness is the loveliest drink in the world,
The loveliest drink in the world, that's what people think in the world!
The other drinks that people drink like rum 'n' scotch 'n' gin,
May be all right upon the night, but sooner or later they do you in!
An' that is a terrible sin! A terrible, terrible sin!

Boozers
But the milk of human kindness is the answer to all the above,
A potion with oceans of love, as cosy an' warm as a glove!
So when you think you need a drink to help you see the sun,
The milk of human kindness is the only one.
Yes, it's the only one!

Tom Jenkins
Before today,
I have to say,
I had no use for milk,
A drink at which I bilk,

	Like others of its ilk!
	An' human kindness also—
	Not at all my cup of tea!
	But put the two together, though,
	An' suddenly I see
Quartet	The perfect drink for me!
	As smooth an' soft as silk!

Boozers	The milk of human kindness
	Is the nicest libation on earth—
	The best celebration on earth—
	The greatest sensation on earth!

Landlord	The other drinks that people drink—
	Like armagnac or port—
Tom Jenkins	May be all right upon the night
	But sooner or later you've drunk a quart!
	Tomorrow you end up in court!
Both	A shockin' an' 'orrible thought!

Even some of the choir are sucked into the celebration

All	But... The Milk of Human Kindness
	Is a source o' salvation for all—
	A nectar for Hector or Paul—
	It's like bein' wrapped in a shawl!
	So any night you choose to booze,
	An' not be on the run—
	The Milk of Human Kindness
	Is the only one,
	Yes, it's the only one!
	Yes, it's the only one!
	Cheers!

Mr Harty has found a Peeler who manages to clear away all the revellers to their homes, revealing a very merry Scrooge

Scrooge	So any night you choose to booze
	Before you see the sun
	The Milk of Human Kindness
	Is the only one
	Yes it's the——

The Ghost of Christmas Present snaps his fingers, leaving Scrooge suddenly sober

The set changes to reveal the kitchen parlour of the Cratchits' house

Scrooge What am I doing in the middle of the street in me nightclothes?
Christmas Present Never mind about your nightclothes. Come. I want you to see the world as it really is.
Scrooge Who lives in this miserable hovel?
Christmas Present Behold the lavish abode of Robert Cratchit, Esquire.
Scrooge (*lamely*) Looks quite nice, really... for a wages clerk... Can I look through the window?
Christmas Present It will cost you nothing, which I'm sure will be good news for you.
Scrooge Will they be able to see me?
Christmas Present No, which I'm sure will be good news for them!
Scrooge I could do with another one of them drinks.
Christmas Present Later. For the time being it's better that you see things as they really are. Touch my robe.

Scrooge does so. There is a blinding flash of light, and Scrooge and Christmas Present are inside the Cratchit family's kitchen-parlour, unseen by them

SCENE 2

The Cratchits' house

Mrs Cratchit, Bob's pretty wife, lifts the lid of the copper and fishes out a rather undernourished muslin-wrapped plum pudding with her copper-stick, sniffs it approvingly and lowers it with loving care back into the bubbling cauldron. Bob Cratchit is carefully assembling and mixing the ingredients for his home-made punch. Three more of the Cratchit children, two boys and a girl, chase one another noisily around the kitchen. Bob finally holds up his hands to silence them

Bob Cratchit (*gently*) Now listen, my dears. Your mother and I want you all to have a good time, but you don't have to wreck the house and kill each other to do it, all right?

The children calm down and nod

Nectar! Pure nectar! And at tuppence a pint you can't really complain.

Martha The stuffing's ready, Mother.

Mrs Cratchit That's lovely, Martha...

Bob promptly sets down his wooden spoon. With immense pride he carries across to the parlour table a crockery platter on which sits the scrawny, poorly plucked goose. The pile of stuffing is bigger than the goose

Bob Cratchit The marriage of roast goose and sage and onion stuffing *a la* Cratchit is one of the culinary miracles of our day—a living legend throughout the length and breadth of Camden Town! (*He sets the platter down upon the table*) The only remaining problem, my dears, is whether to put the stuffing inside the goose or the goose inside the stuffing.

This is greeted with renewed gusts of mirth from the family

But since the ultimate intention is to put them both inside ourselves, I don't suppose it much matters!

Kathy and Tiny Tim enter, looking highly delighted with life

Kathy Come along, Tim.

Bob Cratchit And here they are—the one and only carol-singing Cratchits, newly returned from their triumphant musical tour of Regent's Park and the Euston Road.

The entire family cheers and applauds itself. Bob Cratchit leaves what he is doing, picks up his son and kisses him, and hugs Kathy

Mrs Cratchit How did you do — Tiny Tim?

Tiny Tim Tuppence ha'penny!

Redoubled cheers as he proudly displays his handful of copper coins

Mrs Cratchit Well done! And you too, Kathy!

Bob Cratchit Another fantastic coup by young Timothy Cratchit, the financial wizard! At only seven years of age, the youngest millionaire in the vast Cratchit empire! Let's put the pennies in the jar...

Beautiful Day (No. 15a) starts (underscore)

Mrs Cratchit (*to Kathy*) And how did little Tim behave?

Bob Cratchit sets Tiny Tim on a chair at the parlour table and begins to arrange the pouring of punch into tiny glasses and eggcups

Kathy Good as gold, Mother. When we sang outside the church, he let them see he was a cripple, to remind them at Christmas who made lame beggars walk and blind men see.

Mrs Cratchit He gets thoughtful, sitting by himself so much.

Bob Cratchit Ladies and gentlemen, if I may steal a moment of your valuable time, I would like you to drink to the sparkling good health of the two gentlemen whose industry and generosity have made possible our sumptuous Christmas repast—Master Timothy Cratchit ——

They all raise their glasses

— and Mr Ebenezer Scrooge.

They all lower their glasses. Scrooge mutters a surprised and pleased reaction to the mention of his name in this context—until he sees the smiles fade from the children's faces, and Mrs Cratchit looking at her husband as though he is mad

Mrs Cratchit Mr Scrooge? What are you trying to do—spoil our Christmas?

Bob Cratchit His money paid for the goose, my dear.

Mrs Cratchit No! Your money paid for the goose, my dear.

Bob Cratchit But he paid me the money!

Mrs Cratchit Because you earned it, my love! Believe me! Fifteen shillings a week at threepence an hour, and not a penny rise in eight years. You earned it!

Bob Cratchit Mr Scrooge assures me that times are hard.

Mrs Cratchit He's right. For you, they are! But not for himself!

Bob Cratchit Nonetheless, he is the founder of our feast, and we shall drink to him!

Scrooge (*nodding in agreement*) Quite right!

Mrs Cratchit The founder of our feast, indeed! I wish I had him here! I'd give him a piece of my mind to feast upon, and he'd have indigestion for a month!

Bob Cratchit Ethel, my dear, the children! Christmas!

Mrs Cratchit It needs to be Christmas Day, Bob, to drink to a rotten, stingy old miser like Scrooge!

Scrooge gives the Ghost an embarrassed smile. The Ghost chuckles

Bob Cratchit But, Ethel ——

Mrs Cratchit You know he is, Bob. Nobody knows it better than you, my poor love.

The sparkle seems to have left Bob Cratchit. Tiny Tim hobbles over to him and hands him his glass of punch. Bob touches his wife's hand, smiles at her sadly and raises his glass to her

Bob Cratchit To Christmas, my dear.

Mrs Cratchit Children, we shall drink to your father, for all the love and happiness he gives us, and to Tiny Tim, for the health we wish him... (*She catches Bob's eye*) And for the sake of your father, I'll even drink to that old miser Mr Scrooge. Long life to him, and to us all!

Bob Cratchit A merry Christmas to us all.

Children Merry Christmas.

Bob Cratchit God Bless us.

Tiny Tim God Bless us, every one.

They drink. Bob Cratchit squeezes Tiny Tim's hand

Christmas Present What an unpleasant child! You know, there are few things more nauseating than a happy family enjoying themselves at Christmas! Do you not agree, Scrooge?

Scrooge I think Bob Cratchit's really rather fond of me!

The Ghost roars with laughter

Christmas Present So's his wife! Couldn't you tell?

Scrooge She doesn't really know me.

Christmas Present That is one of the few things wherein Fate has blessed her.

Bob Cratchit As I said to the Lord Mayor, if Her Most Gracious Majesty is feeling bored, I said, you just wheel her over to Camden Town, I said! We'll have her back on her regal feet in no time, I said, with a glass of Bob Cratchit's hot punch ... and a song from young Tiny Tim.

All heads turn to Tiny Tim. Tim blushes, but finally responds to the vociferous urging of his brothers and sisters. Bob Cratchit lifts him up to stand on the table. The family cheers and applauds. Everyone falls silent

No. 16: The Beautiful Day

Tiny Tim   On a beautiful day
                       That I dream about
                       In a world I would love to see

>Is a beautiful place
>Where the sun comes out—
>And it shines in the sky for me.
>
>On this beautiful winter's morning,
>If my wish could come true
>Somehow,
>Then the beautiful day
>That I dream about
>Would be here
>And now.

Tiny Tim continues singing sotto voce under the following scene between Scrooge and Christmas Present who continue their dialogue

>On a beautiful day
>That I dream about
>In a world I would love to see
>
>Is a beautiful place
>Where the sun comes out—
>And the sun shines in the sky for me.
>
>On this beautiful winter's morning,
>If my wish could come true
>Somehow,
>
>Then the beautiful day
>That I dream about
>Would be here,
>And now.

Scrooge wipes a tear from the corner of his eye as they walk away

Scrooge What will become of him... Tiny Tim?

Christmas Present What's this? Concern over a sick child? Have you taken leave of your senses?

Scrooge Don't mock me, Spirit. Is the child very sick? Not that it's of any great importance to me whether he is or not... but is he?

Christmas Present Well, of course he's sick!

Scrooge You mean he's seriously ill? Will he ... live?

Christmas Present stares caustically down at Scrooge who gets angry

Well, will he?

Christmas Present What does it matter to you, Ebenezer Scrooge? If he is going to die, then he had better do it, and decrease...

Both ... the surplus population!

Scrooge hangs his head to hear his own words quoted. Focus back to the Cratchits for the end of the song

Cratchits   Then the beautiful day that I dream about
                            Would be here and now.

Christmas Present Of course the boy will die! Unless the future changes in an unforeseen fashion. But who are you to decide who is surplus? I suspect there are many of the opinion that it is *you* who are surplus!

Scrooge I should like to go home now.

Christmas Present No. We have one last call to make. Touch my robe.

As the Cratchits end the refrain The Beautiful Day, Scrooge touches Christmas Present's robe. There is a blinding flash of light

I Like Life (No. 16a) starts (underscore)

SCENE 3

Scrooge's Nephew's sitting-room

A warm, cosy Christmas, the room illuminated by firelight and candle-glow

As the Lights cross-fade, there is a contrasting, uplifting swirl of music, and a tumble of rowdy, happy Children in bright party clothes bounce across the stage to the music of I Like Life. *They are playing Blind Man's Buff, laughing, giggling and screaming with delight. The Adults follow, among them Scrooge's nephew, Harry, and his pretty wife, Helen (played by the same actress who was Isabel, whom Scrooge never quite sees). Blindfolded is Harry's best friend, Topper. As he gropes and stumbles about, he always seems to seek out the same attractive and buxom lady, named Mary*

Helen I think Topper can see through that blindfold! He keeps chasing Mary!

Nephew Well, you can't blame him, can you?

Helen Oh Harry, you're outrageous!

Topper makes a final lunge for Mary and grabs her in an elaborate embrace. Mary whips off his blindfold

Topper (*in mock surprise*) Good heavens! Mary, it's you!

Helen Right! Mary and Topper, you choose the next game. Harry, you top up everyone's glasses. Grown-ups all stay here! Children follow me! Hot mince pies and milk in the nursery!

The Children cheer and follow Helen like the Pied Piper

Harry refills the drinks. The Ghost of Christmas Present sits on a large sofa and beckons Scrooge to sit beside him. Scrooge hesitates

Christmas Present Come on, Scrooge! It's all right! I'm the Guest of Honour! (*He points to himself*) Christmas!

Scrooge sits down

Nephew Ladies and gentlemen, will you please honour me with your undivided attention? That famous moment has arrived that I know you all look forward to in this house every Christmas Eve, when I ask you to drink to the good health and long life of my celebrated Uncle Ebenezer!

The Friends respond to the proposal—albeit with no great show of enthusiasm—and toast Scrooge. Scrooge's face lights up. He nudges the Ghost

Scrooge Did you hear that? Maybe I've misjudged the boy.

Topper Harry, I've visited you every Christmas for the past five years, and to this day I can never understand this extraordinary ritual of drinking to the health of your Uncle Ebenezer! Everybody knows he's the most miserable old skinflint that ever walked God's earth!

Guests Hear, hear...

Scrooge Who's he?

Christmas Present Oh, just a friend.

Nephew My dear Topper, it's very simple. He is indeed the most despicable old miser — worse than you could ever possibly imagine ——

The Ghost chuckles

Scrooge You find this amusing?

Christmas Present Believe it or not, he likes you!

Nephew But I look at it this way—if I can wish a merry Christmas to him, who is beyond dispute the most obnoxious and parsimonious of all living creatures ——

Guests Hear, hear!

Christmas Present is helpless with laughter

Nephew ...then I know in my heart I am truly a man of goodwill!
Scrooge The scoundrel!
Topper Now that I'll drink to!

Scrooge, beside himself, goes over to Topper and glares at him

Scrooge I don't like *you* at all!
Christmas Present Wait, there is more to come!
Nephew Besides, I like old Scrooge.

Scrooge perks up

Christmas Present What did I tell you?
Guests Nonsense...! Oh no...!
Nephew I truly do! God knows, I have little enough reason to do so after the way he treated our family, but I can't help feeling that hidden somewhere inside that loathsome old carcass of his... there is a different man fighting to get out!
Topper Careful, Harry—he may be even worse than the one you know!

Laughter from everyone except Scrooge

Nephew God forbid! Anyway, that's why I invite him to come here every Christmas, in the forlorn hope that one day he might just drop by and pick up enough goodwill to raise his clerk's wages by five shillings a week! God knows, it's high time he did!
Guests Hear, hear! Bravo!
Scrooge You're very free with other people's money.
Mary All right, Harry, now that's enough! I refuse to have my Christmas haunted by your silly old Uncle Ebenezer!

Scrooge finds this amusing

Scrooge If only you knew, my dear! (*He walks over to her, shrieks a mock ghostly shriek and pulls a face at her*)

Christmas Present roars with laughter

Mary All right, what shall we play?
Lizzi Charades...
Lucy Secrets...

Stuart Sardines...
Charles Murder...
Sarah Hunt the Thimble...
Topper Postman's Knock...
Mary I know—we'll all sing *The Minister's Cat.*

Approval from the Guests

No. 17: The Minister's Cat

Scrooge As for you, Nephew, if you were in my will, which you're not,
  I'd disinherit you. Raise my clerk's wages! Humbug!
Christmas Present Scrooge, come over here. You need some more of this.
  (*He produces a silver goblet out of nowhere and pours a drink*)

*Scrooge brightens up immediately and sits on the sofa next to Christmas
Present. The music begins*

Scrooge I know that tune! I used to sing it when I was at old Fezziwig's!
  Ti-tum, ti-tum, ti-tum, ti-tum...

*Christmas Present nods approvingly, and munches an oversized leg of
turkey, waving it like a conductor's baton as he watches Scrooge*

Mary All right. I'll conduct. Now remember, one line each. Let's see if we
  can get through the whole alphabet without a mistake. Ready, steady, A!

*Mary calls out at the start of each line "A... B... C..." etc, and points to a
Guest who has to sing in turn, one line each*

Guests   (*singing*) The minister's cat is an Affable cat.
                The minister's cat is a Boring cat.
                The minister's cat is a Charming cat.
                At one o'clock on a Monday.

                The minister's cat is a Darling cat.
                The minister's cat is an Evil cat.
                The minister's cat is a Frightful cat.
                At two o'clock on a Tuesday.

                The minister's cat is a Grumpy cat.
                The minister's cat is a Hungry cat.
                The minister's cat is an Idiot cat.
                At three o'clock on a Wednesday.

> The minister's cat is a Jealous cat.
> The minister's cat is a Kindly cat.
> The minister's cat is a Lonely cat.
> At four o'clock on a Thursday.

Nephew (*speaking*) The minister's cat is a mmmm ... er... M ... M... Oh gosh!
Scrooge (*yelling*) Merry! Say merry!

The music keeps the tempo going while the Guests hold their breath or giggle in delight

Mary You've got three seconds ... three ... two ... one...
Nephew (*floundering*) Mi ... ma ... mem... (*Furious with himself*) Aaaaagh!
Mary You're out! Right—keep it going! N!
Guests (*continuing in turn*) The minister's cat is a Naughty cat.
>   The minister's cat is an Oval cat.
>   At five o'clock on a Friday.

Harry, laughing, steps out of the circle, and pours himself a glass of port. Scrooge, deeply caught up in the game, follows him. The song continues under the following

Scrooge (*furiously*) I told you to say "merry"! What's the matter with you? Why are you so stupid!? (*To Christmas Present*) He's always been stupid. (*To Harry*) You could have said merry, or monstrous, or miserable, monastic, maniacal, moronic... That's what you are—moronic!
Nephew Moronic!
Guests   The minister's cat is a Perfect cat.
>   The minister's cat is a Quirky cat.
>   The minister's cat is a Reverent cat.
>   At six o'clock on a Saturday.
>
>   The minister's cat is a Silky cat.
>   The minister's cat is a Tiresome cat.
>   The minister's cat is a Useless cat.
>   At seven o'clock on a Sunday.
Scrooge Useless, that's what you are, useless...

Scrooge joins in as the song builds to a climax, singing just the adjective for each letter. He is the centre-piece of the song's finish

The minister's cat is a Vicious cat.
The minister's cat is a Worldly cat.
The minister's cat is an X-traordinary cat.
A Yellow-eyed cat.
A Zippy Zany Zanzibar cat.

Mary   And what do you make of all that?

All   We'll tell you what we make of that!
                  The minister truly, truly has
                  An absolutely most remarkable cat!

The company bursts into a roar of self-congratulatory applause and delight at their achievement. Scrooge joins in

December the Twenty-Fifth (No. 17a) continues (underscore)

Scrooge Wonderful! Absolutely marvellous! My word, that was lots of fun. We used to sing that at old Fezziwig's parties... (*To Harry*) I can't believe how stupid you are!
Topper Harry, lovely evening. It's late. We must go. Christmas in the morning.
Scrooge No, no, no! Don't go! Must you really? Oh, dear...

The Guests take their leave. Scrooge lines up with the hosts, chatting amiably as he bids the Guests farewell during the following

Helen reappears with the by-now sleepy Children, a large basket of presents draped over her arm. She hands a gift-wrapped little package to each Guest as they leave

Harry, unaware of Scrooge, continues to chat to his Guests during Scrooge's speech. The furniture is cleared away

Going already? What a pity! But it was a wonderful evening! And I loved that Minister's Cat thing—I thought I was rather good at it! Good-night... Good-night ... Thank you for coming ... I can honestly say I haven't enjoyed a Christmas as much as this since I was a young apprentice at old Fezziwig's—oh, so many years ago... What Christmasses we used to have in those days! Fantastic, they were ... He had this daughter...
Nephew ...Good-night, Mary.
Mary Good-night.
Nephew Merry Christmas, Topper—I'll try to get Uncle Ebenezer here for you next year!

Topper Don't bother!
Scrooge (*as Topper passes*) I really don't like you at all!
Nephew (*waving*) Merry Christmas, everybody.
Guests Merry Christmas!

The Guests leave

Happiness (Reprise) (No. 18) starts (underscore)

Christmas Present gently leads Scrooge away from the party. The Guests fade from view, the sound of their laughter drifting off into the darkness

Harry and Helen waltz off together to the music of "Happiness"

The Lights cross-fade to:

SCENE 4

Scrooge's bedroom

Scrooge continues talking, moved by his memories. He does not realize where he is. His thoughts are far away from this time and place. His eyes fill with tears as he speaks

For a few moments we see Isabel and Ebenezer together, young again, like Scrooge's voice as he remembers this happy time gone by

The music of "Happiness" continues to play gently under. Scrooge looks around him vaguely, as the bedroom re-forms around him

Scrooge (*singing*) Happiness was standing beside me...
                          I could see her...
                          She could see me...
                          Happiness can be something you're too blind to see...

(*Speaking*) Oh, Isabel...!

Music 18a: Happiness (Underscore)

Ebenezer and Isabel fade from view. Scrooge's voice trails away as he sees Christmas Present beside him, back in the bedroom

Christmas Present Scrooge, my time upon this little planet is very brief. I must leave you now.

Scrooge But we still have so much to talk about! Haven't we?

Christmas Present There is never enough time to say or do all the things we would wish. The thing is to try to do as much as you can with the time that you have.

A Better Life (No. 19) continues (underscore)

Scrooge Oh, just one more drink...

As Christmas Present speaks, his voice and his form vanish simultaneously

Christmas Present (*walking away*) Remember, Scrooge, time is short, and suddenly you're not there any more...

Scrooge shivers, and looks about him in the gloom

Scrooge No, wait! Don't go... Don't leave me... Where are you? Why is it so dark? I can't see... I can't see...

> (*Singing*) Do my eyes deceive me?
> Can my reason lie?
> Am I living here and now?
> Or in some life-gone-by?
>
> Is this world I'm seeing
> The world I saw before?
> Could there be another life?
> That might have taught me more?
>
> Am I merely dreaming?
> Or am I awake?
> Is my mind just playing games?
> Or showing me
> A pathway I should take?
>
> Do I just ignore it?
> Do I break the spell?
> Or do I take another look?
> Open up a brand-new book?
>
> Try to find a better life?
> A bigger, brighter, better life?
> And could I somehow learn
> To live it well?

> Only time ... only time ... will tell!
> Can I find a better life—
> And learn to live it well?

The music continues under as Scrooge hears voices from his past

Isabel's Voice If you met me today you would not love me, Ebenezer.
Bob Cratchit's Voice Can I have my wages please, Mr Scrooge?
The Ghost of Christmas Past's Voice Love is life's greatest gift, Ebby;
never hide your love from those you cherish.

Scrooge   Dare I just ignore it?
Dare I break the spell?
Or dare I take another look?
Open up a brand-new book—
Try to find a better life—
A bigger, brighter, better life—
And maybe even hope
To live it well?
Only time ... only time ... will tell...

Is there time to get a life?
To find myself a better life?
And learn to live it well!

The church clock starts to chime three o 'clock in the distance. Macabre and ghostly sounds fill the night. Scrooge buries his face in his hands, a man totally in the grip of terror

(*Speaking*) Three o'clock... "The third at three". (*He looks up, startled*)

Looming over him is a shapeless black Phantom—a fearsome sight

Scrooge gulps and closes his eyes. The Phantom is immobile

Am I in the presence of The Ghost of Christmas Yet-to-Come? And are you to show me shadows of the things that will happen in the time before us?

The Phantom nods. Scrooge closes his eyes, summoning up his final reserves of inner strength

Ghost of the Future! I fear you more than any apparition I have ever seen. But as I know your purpose is to do me good, and as I hope to live to be another man from what I was, I am prepared to bear you company. Will you speak to me?

Still the Phantom gives no reply, but lifts one of its shrouded arms and points towards the window out into the night. Scrooge nods timidly and scrambles after him, nightcap askew

The night is waning fast, and I know it is precious time to me. Lead on, Spirit, lead on!

The Phantom raises both arms skyward. Thunder and lightning fill the night sky. A howling, icy gale blows through the room. Scrooge stands shivering in his long nightgown, his teeth chattering with a combination of cold and terror. The force of the wind increases until it is a typhoon. With a wild cry of fear, Scrooge is whirled around until he is dizzy

The Lights cross-fade to:

Scene 5

The street outside Scrooge's office

Scrooge stands beside the Phantom, slightly removed from a crowd of people gathered outside his office. Tom Jenkins polishes the gleaming brass "Scrooge & Marley" nameplate with his shirt-sleeve

Tom Jenkins There it is, friends, shinin' as bright as the 'appy thoughts the mere mention of the name Scrooge brings to our minds! (*Addressing the Crowd*) Ladies and gentlemen. We are gathered 'ere today because we are united by a common bond——

The Crowd raises a cheer

——namely our feelings of gratitude to Mr Ebenezer Scrooge.

The Crowd roars its raucous agreement

I don't think any one of us could ever' ope to find the words to describe the true depth of our feelings towards 'im!
Scrooge (*to the Phantom*) Is this the future?

The Phantom nods. It is clear that Scrooge, already in a highly emotional condition, is deeply touched. He starts to move among the Crowd

Tom Jenkins (*quietening the mob*) All right, now, my friends, settle down, if you please.

Scrooge That's Tom Jenkins ... the hot soup man. Owes me six pounds. I must say he looks uncommonly happy for a man so deep in debt.

Tom Jenkins I completely understand 'ow emotional you all feel about this most important celebration...

Another rousing cheer from the Crowd. Scrooge observes in the Crowd the smiling faces of the Punch and Judy Man, and the Dilbers, who run the knitwear stall, and others

Scrooge All these people owe me money. They love me, and I never knew.

Tom Jenkins But may I ask you to kindly 'old yer emotions in check. We are all deeply moved, and those of us what have been in debt to Mr S over the years will never forget the rare and beautiful thing 'E's just done for all of us, right?

Crowd Right!

The Crowd cheers. Scrooge is delighted at the Crowd's reaction, and questions them, forgetting they can neither see nor hear him

Scrooge What did I do? What did I do? Whatever it was, it has made them truly happy. And I am the cause!

Tom Jenkins puts up his hands for silence as he enters the office

Scrooge steps up on to the mounting block in front of his office to address the Crowd

No. 20: Thank You Very Much

Ladies and gentlemen... I thank you from the bottom of my heart! I shall remember this moment until my dying day!

> (*Singing*) May I say to all my friends
> Who have assembled here,
> That I'd merely like to mention, if I may,
> My sincere and humble attitude
> Is one of lasting gratitude
> For what your words
> Have done for me today!
> And therefore I would simply like to say...

Tom Jenkins comes out of the office and produces Scrooge's black note-book, from which he proceeds to tear the pages, tossing them into the air

The Crowd's cheers of appreciation coincide with Scrooge's singing

Scrooge   Thank you very much!
                            Thank you very much!
                            That's the nicest thing
                            That anyone's ever done for me!
                            I may sound double-dutch,
                            But my delight is such
                            I feel as if a losing war's
                            Been won for me!

                            And if I had a flag
                            I'd hang me flag out—
                            To add a sort of final victory touch!
                            But since I left me flag at home
                            I'll simply have to say
                            Thank you very, very, very much!

At a gesture from Tom Jenkins, four Men emerge from Scrooge's office carrying a coffin which they dump heavily and unceremoniously next to the unseen Scrooge

This produces a great roar of approval from the Crowd, Scrooge, wallowing in the Crowd's apparent affection for him, does not notice the coffin

Scrooge
Tom Jenkins   } *(together)* Thank you very, very, very much!
Crowd

Cheers from the Crowd around him. Tom Jenkins jumps up and dances on Scrooge's coffin, Scrooge, unaware of the situation, is having a wonderful time

The Dilbers run into the house

Scrooge   Thank you very much!
                            Thank you very much!
                            That's the nicest thing
                            That anyone's ever done for me!

It sounds a bit bizarre,
But things the way they are
I feel as if another life's
Begun for me!

And if I had a cannon
I would fire it—
To add a sort of celebration touch!
But since I left me cannon at home
I'll simply have to say
Thank you very, very, very much!

Company   Thank you very, very, very much!

From the upper window of Scrooge's lodgings, the Dilbers happily throw Scrooge's possessions down into the street for everyone to help themselves

MrsDilber Oi!

Scrooge }   Thank you very much!
Company }   Thank you very much!
                    That's the nicest thing
                    That anyone's ever done for me!
                    It isn't every day
                    Good fortune comes me way!
                    I never thought the future would be fun for me.

A Woman shouts down from an upper window

Woman (*speaking*) Will you be quiet?! My baby's tryin' ter sleep!
Scrooge (*speaking*) I'm terrible sorry, Madam...

Scrooge }   (*in hushed voices*) An' if I 'ad a bugle
Company }   I would blow it—
                    To add a sort of 'ow's-yer-father touch!
                    But since I left me bugle at 'ome
                    I'll simply 'ave ter say
                    Thank you very, very, very much!

Scrooge (*speaking*) No, my dear friends! It is *I* who should be grateful to *you*!

Company   For 'e's a jolly good fellow!
                    For 'e's a jolly good fellow!
Scrooge   For I'm a jolly good fellow!
Company   And so say all of us!

Scrooge   Thank you very much! **Tom Jenkins** Thank you very much!
Thank you very much!   **and Company** Thank you very much!
That's the nicest thing   Thank you very, very much!
That anyone's ever done for me   Thank you very much!
The future looks all right   Thank you very much!
In fact it looks so bright   Thank you very much!
I feel as if they're   Thank you very much!
Polishing the sun for me!   Very, very much!

Scrooge ⎫   And if I 'ad a drum
Company ⎬   I'd 'ave to bang it!

Company   To add a sort of rumpty-tumpty touch!
But since I left me drummer at 'ome—
I'll simply 'ave ter say
Thank you very, very, very much
Thank you very, very, very:
He's a jolly good fellow:
Thank you very much!

Willing hands heave Scrooge's coffin merrily up on to a handcart. The Crowd moves off, pulling the handcart, cheering, with Tom Jenkins dancing round it

Scrooge, in a very good mood, hums Thank You Very Much *to himself*

Scrooge Spirit, I shall not forget this lesson, trust me. May I go home now?

The Phantom shakes his head and then points upstage. Scrooge turns

The Lights cross-fade to:

Scene 6

No. 21: The Beautiful Day (Reprise) starts underscore

The Cratchits' house

Scrooge Bob Cratchit's house. Why have we come here again?

Mrs Cratchit and the Children are seated around the kitchen table. The parlour is half-heartedly prepared for Christmas, and the sadness in the faces of the Cratchits is in depressing contrast to Scrooge's previous visit.

Mrs Cratchit and her daughters are sewing, while Peter is reading a book. Mrs Cratchit lays her work on the table, and puts her hand up to her face

Kathy Mother?
Mrs Cratchit The colour hurts my eyes, and I mustn't show weak eyes to your father when he gets home. It must be near his time.
Kathy Past it. But I think he has walked a little slower these past few evenings.

They are all very quiet again. At last Mrs Cratchit speaks in a steady, cheerful voice, that only falters once

Mrs Cratchit I have known him to walk with Tiny Tim upon his shoulder very fast indeed.
Kathy So have I. Often.
Mrs Cratchit But he was light to carry, and his father loved him. So it was no trouble ... no trouble.

Scrooge looks at the empty chair which Tiny Tim previously occupied

Scrooge There is Tiny Tim's chair. But there is no Tiny Tim. (*He stares coldly at the Phantom*) Where is he?

The Phantom leads Scrooge off

The Lights cross-fade to:

SCENE 7

The churchyard

The Phantom leads Scrooge to a simple graveyard, a bleak aspect of cold grey and black stone against a sombre slate sky

Bob Cratchit is kneeling in front of a simple white wooden cross. The only splash of colour in the graveyard is the bunch of violets in his hands. He is infinitely sad, but he keeps a brave face in front of Tiny Tim. He places the bunch of violets at the foot of the white cross, which is simply inscribed "Timothy Cratchit, 1837-1844—Aged 7 years"

We faintly hear a voice-over of Tiny Tim singing the song he sang for his family the previous Christmas

No. 21: The Beautiful Day (*Reprise*)

Tiny Tim (*voice-over*) On a beautiful day
That I dream about
In a world I would love to see...

Bob Cratchit (*speaking*) I must go now, my little fellow. I promised your
mother I'd help her with the Christmas dinner, but I'll come and see you
again tomorrow ... same time, all right?

(*Singing*) On this beautiful winter's morning,
If my wish could come true
Somehow
Then the beautiful day
That I dream about
Would be here
And...

(*Speaking*) Oh, Tim!

*His voice breaks, and for a moment he bows his head, too heartbroken
to move. Then he pulls himself together, attempts his usual cheery smile
and clambers to his feet*

*With a last sad look at the pathetic little grave, Bob Cratchit hurries
away*

Scrooge (*watching him go*) Poor Tiny Tim! Spirit, you have shown me a
Christmas yet to come that mingles great happiness with great sadness.
Answer me one question. Are these the shadows of things that will be, or
are they shadows of things that may be, only?

*For answer, the Phantom points up to a large, grey, flat slab or stone near
Tiny Tim's grave, previously obscured in the gloom. Now clearly visible on
it are the words EBENEZER SCROOGE. Scrooge utters a strangled cry. His
face fills with terror as he hears a familiar voice calling him*

Scrooge Ahhhhhh!

*He turns back in horror to the Phantom, who points from Scrooge to the grave
and then advances slowly towards him. Scrooge backs away, mesmerized
with fear, his voice a hoarse whisper*

Spirit! If you are indeed here to show me the errors of my past ways, tell me. So that I may, by my good deeds, sponge away the writing on this dreaded stone!

Marley appears to greet him, his hand extended, a thin welcoming smile on his gaunt face, his fearful chain clanking behind him

Marley Ebenezer Scrooge! We've been expecting you! You're early! Not that it matters in eternity. They apologize that your chain wasn't ready for your arrival, but it's so big they had to take on extra little devils at the foundry to finish it!

Four shadowy figures approach them, bent double and groaning beneath the mighty weight of Scrooge's gigantic chain

Ah, here it is now! It's even bigger than I thought it would be! My word, makes mine look like a watch chain!

Scrooge Oh, Sweet Spirit! Hear me, I pray you! I am not the man I was! I vow I will honour Christmas in my heart, and keep it every day of the year! I swear it! Only spare me, that I may live to prove it!

Marley Bah! Humbug! Merry Christmas, Ebenezer Scrooge!

Marley laughs as the Phantoms and the huge chain bear down on Scrooge

Scrooge Spirit, help me! (*He clutches desperately at the black shrouded figure of the Ghost, pulling the winding-sheet from him*)

The Ghost emits a spine-chilling banshee wail as he spins away from Scrooge, melts through the floor and vanishes

The Lights darken on the flailing figure of Scrooge. He continues to cry for help. His voice echoes and re-echoes away into the darkness as Hell disintegrates around him. The Lights cross-fade to:

SCENE 8

Scrooge's bedroom

His bed magically returns to him as the Lights come up. Scrooge, heavily entangled in sheets and blankets, is fighting to free himself

Scrooge Where am I? I'm my own room I'm not dead! (*He throws off the sheets*)

No. 22: I'll Begin Again

Perhaps it didn't happen after all... perhaps it did... But I'm alive! I've got a chance to change, and I will not be the man I was!

The music builds under

> (*Singing*) I'll begin again
> I will build my life.
> I will live to know
> That I've fulfilled my life.
> I'll begin today—
> Throw away the past—
> And the future I build
> Will be something that will last.
>
> I will take the time
> I have left to live,
> And I'll give it all
> That I have left to give.
>
> I will live my days
> For my fellow men,
> And I'll live in praise
> Of that moment when
> I was able to begin again!

I don't know what to do. I'm as light as a feather. I'm as happy as an angel. I'm as giddy as a drunken man. Oh, Jacob Marley, wherever you are, you shall see a change in me, I swear! A merry Christmas everybody! Merry Christmas!

He throws back the curtains and looks out at the world, a new man. Daylight floods into the room. He puts on his dressing-gown and bedroom slippers, and moves downstage. The bedroom dissolves behind him and he steps into the blinding light of a dazzling new day. He drinks in the glorious morning

> I'll begin again
> I will change my fate!
> I will show the world
> That it is not too late!
> I will never stop—
> While I still have time—

> Till I stand at the top
> Of that mountain I must climb!

*The Ghosts of Marley, Christmas Past and Present are seen through
Scrooge's mirror, nodding approval*

> I will start anew.
> I will make amends.
> And I'll make quite certain
> That the story ends
> On a note of hope—
> On a strong amen—
> And I'll thank the world
> And remember when
> I was able to begin again!
> I'll begin again!

*Scrooge, still in his nightclothes, stands in the middle of the street, laughing
and crying with joy. The church bells merrily chime nine o'clock*

The Lights cross-fade to:

SCENE 9

A London street—Cheapside

*A small boy trudges through the snow along the street. He stops and stares
in amazement at Scrooge in his nightclothes*

Scrooge Boy... Boy! What day is it?
Boy Today? Why, Christmas Day, o' course!
Scrooge (*letting out a bellow of triumph and clapping his hands*) It's
Christmas Day! I haven't missed it!

Christmas Children (No. 22a) starts (underscore)

(*He turns back to the boy*) Do you know the butcher's shop in the next
street but one?
Boy I should 'ope so!
Scrooge What an intelligent boy! A remarkable boy! Do you happen to
know whether they've sold the prize turkey that was hanging up in the
window? Not the big one—the enormous one!
Boy You mean the one as big as me?

Scrooge What a delightful boy! So witty! It's a pleasure to talk to him! That's the one!

Boy It's still there.

Scrooge It is? Go and buy it.

Boy Wassat?

Scrooge Here's two sovereigns. Go and wake up the butcher and have him open up his shop. Meet me there in five minutes. Be holding that turkey, and I'll give you tuppence — sixpence — a shilling ... I'll give you half a crown! Go on, run — run — run!

The Boy disappears like a shot

Scrooge chuckles

Oh, what a lovely boy! I think I'm going to like children. *(He hurries next door to the toy shop and bangs on the door)*

The toy shop owner, Mr Pringle, his face covered in shaving cream, emerges and stares at Scrooge in a state of shock. His wife follows, equally dumbfounded

Pringle Mr Scrooge?

Scrooge Good-morning, Pringle. A merry Christmas to you. I want some toys—lots of toys—for all my young friends on this joyous day.

Pringle T-t-toys?! *You*, Mr Scrooge?

Scrooge Yes. Well, don't stand there gaping, man—make a list.

Pringle A list. Yes. Of course, Mr Scrooge.

Scrooge *(pointing at the carousel)* I want that and that and that. And two of those and the hobby horse and some flutes—some trumpets, oh, and that doll in the corner, and some bows and arrows!

Pringle *(dumbfounded)* Bows and arrows...

Scrooge Oh yes, I must have a cricket bat, and these, and that horse and this piano... I like that, oh, and this beautiful coach and several kites and these boats and some of these and I'll have that...

The traumatized Pringle scribbles at great speed, trying to keep up with Scrooge's dizzying selections. His small Boy Assistant is wide-eyed with wonder at the miracle he is witnessing. Mrs Pringle watches in amazement

Pringle Y-yes, Mr Scrooge.

Scrooge And how much is all that?

Pringle I—I—I... how much? Er...
Scrooge Never mind. Here are some sovereigns. You can keep the change.

Mr Pringle clutches the door and Mrs Pringle for support

Pringle I... er... Th—thank you, Mr Scrooge.
Scrooge And I shall require the services of several small boys—to help carry it all! Each boy will receive half a crown!
Mrs Pringle Half a—yes, Mr Scrooge!

A radiant Scrooge emerges from the toy shop to be met by Bissett, the Butcher, and the Boy, who is almost totally obscured by the gigantic turkey he is carrying

Scrooge That's what I call a turkey! It's twice the size of Tiny Tim! Come along, dear boy—thank you. Merry Christmas!
Bissett But Mr Scrooge—what's happened?
Scrooge What's happened? It's perfectly simple, Bissett. I've discovered that ... I ... like ... life!

An ever-strengthening musical undercurrent—No. 23a, the prelude to the extended musical finale that is to come—begins to build from this point. The dumbfounded Bissett, still half-asleep, turns to Mr Pringle in wonderment

Bissett That *was* old Scrooge, wasn't it?

They follow Scrooge in disbelief at what they are witnessing. Scrooge begins an eccentric, Pied-Piper-like procession through the streets of Cheapside

No. 23: Finale Act II

As Scrooge sings, Mr Pringle and his Assistants bring out a succession of gift-wrapped packages, while the Boy organizes the open-mouthed Urchins to provide handcarts to transport the mountain of purchases. Passers-by stop to stare in amazement at the scene

Scrooge   I like Life! Life likes me!
                               Life and I very fully agree
                               Life is fine! Life is good!
                               'Specially mine,
                               Which is just as it should be!

Scrooge shops as he sings. He chooses several cases of wine from the astonished Wine Merchant

> I like pouring the wine— (*he does so*)
> And why not? (*He tastes and approves it*)
> Life's a pleasure
> That I deny not!

He hands bottles of wine at random to various Onlookers. The spirit of Christmas builds around him as the song progresses

Two portly Gentlemen, Jollygoode and Harty, approach

Scrooge Ah, Mr Harty! And Mr Jollygoode! Good-day, gentlemen. Merry Christmas!

Jollygoode/Harty (*caught off guard*) Er... Merry Christmas, Mr Scrooge.

Scrooge Come to my office on Monday morning and I will give you one hundred guineas for your most worthy cause! And the same every Christmas!

The Crowd cheers as the two Gentlemen look appropriately staggered

Jollygoode B-b-but, Mr Scrooge... Why?

Scrooge For a jolly good reason, Mr Jollygoode! (*He points to the Crowd*) They will tell you why. Excuse me!

Scrooge giggles and dances away into a Christmas gift store as the happy Crowd sings to Harty and Jollygoode

Butcher ⎤ **Pringle** ⎦	I like life! Here and now! Life and I made a mutual vow— Till I die, Life and I— We'll both try To be better somehow!
Company	Where there's music and laughter, Happiness is rife!
Jollygoode	Why? Because I like life!

A roar goes up as Scrooge emerges from the clothing shop, resplendent in a Santa Claus outfit. He hands his sack to the Urchins

Jollygoode/Harty (*in total shock*) I don't believe it!

Scrooge	Farver Chris'mas!
Urchins ⎤ **Scrooge** ⎦	Farver Chris'mas!

Urchins, Scrooge	'E's the greatest man
and Ladies	In the 'ole wide world!
	In the 'ole wide world!
	An' 'e knows it!
Company	Every Chris'mas
	Farver Chris'mas

Scrooge takes the sack back from the Urchins

> Puts a great big sack
> On 'is dear old back—
> 'Cos 'e loves us all—
> An' 'e shows it!

They push Scrooge on to a sled and pull him around the stage

Company   An' 'e goes
                     For a sleigh-ride
                     If it snows
                     Then 'e may ride all night!
                     But that's all right!

                     In the mornin'—
                     Christmas mornin'—
                     If yer lift yer eyes,
                     There's a big surprise!
                     On yer bed you'll see
                     There's a gift from Farver Chris'mas—
                     From Farver Chris'mas—
                     That's 'ow Chris'mas oughta be!

Scene 10

The Cratchits' house

The procession swirls around Scrooge

Scrooge (*unseen*) Ho ho ho!

The procession suddenly parts to reveal the assembled Cratchit family. The Cratchit Children are a-tremble with excitement at the sight of Santa Claus. Cratchit's jaw drops open when he sees Scrooge and his followers. But there is no glimmer of recognition of his employer

Scrooge Robert Cratchit, Esquire?

Bob Cratchit nods dumbly

A merry Christmas to you, sir, from Santa Claus himself!
Bob Cratchit Forgive me, sir, but I think you've got the wrong people.
Scrooge Nonsense! I haven't gone to the wrong people in eighteen hundred
   and forty-three years! (*He grabs the huge turkey from the Boy and turns
   to Mrs Cratchit. Briskly*) Don't worry about that scrawny little goose of
   yours, Mrs Cratchit! You can use it as stuffing for this! (*He dumps the giant
   turkey in her arms, nearly knocking her off her feet*)
Mrs Cratchit (*amazed*) Thank you, sir! But how did you know about...?
Scrooge (*ignoring her*) Now, where are the other presents—the ones for the
   children?

*Several Children in his retinue promptly step forward and Scrooge showers
several gifts on four of the Cratchit children, chattering away all the time*

This is for you, my dear ... and this one is for you. (*To Kathy*) And this
   pretty doll is for you.
Kathy It's the dolly in the corner!
Scrooge And those are for you, my boy.
Peter Thank you, sir.
Scrooge And these, Bob Cratchit, are for yourself and your good lady
   wife.

*He presents the catatonic Cratchits with two leather purses, each jingling
with gold sovereigns. The whole family is struck dumb by the onslaught.
Scrooge chuckles and rubs his hands gleefully*

Well, I must leave you now. As you may imagine, this is an extremely busy
   day for me, and I have many other calls to make! (*He turns to go*)

*Tiny Tim, the only one of the family who hasn't received a present, is too
disappointed to utter. Then Scrooge turns back. He kneels down in front of
the giftless Tiny Tim and looks at him tenderly*

Oh, I almost forgot. This is for you!

*At the snap of the fingers from Scrooge, two Children place the last and the
largest of the packages on the floor in front of Tiny Tim. Scrooge lifts off the
wrapping that covers it, revealing the carousel that was the centrepiece of the
toyshop window. It is a hundred gifts in one, comprising animals and toys and
sweets of every kind. Tiny Tim is awestruck but practical*

Tiny Tim You didn't steal it, did you?
Scrooge (*chuckling*) A merry Christmas, Tiny Tim!

Tiny Tim puts his arms around Scrooge's neck and hugs him. Scrooge, deeply moved, kisses the child on the cheek then bounces back to his feet, smiling from ear to ear

You still don't recognize me, do you, Bob Cratchit?
Bob Cratchit (*nodding and shaking his head in total confusion*) Yes, no—I mean—you're Father Christmas!

Scrooge throws back his head and roars with laughter, utterly delighted. With a flourish he pulls his beard and whiskers off. Mrs Cratchit and her three daughters scream in unison

Mrs Cratchit It's Mr Scrooge! He's gone mad!
Bob Cratchit It's all right, dear—there's nothing to be afraid of!
Scrooge No, I haven't gone mad! And on Monday, when your salary will be doubled——
Bob Cratchit He *has* gone mad!
Scrooge —we'll sit together and discuss what I can do to help your family. To start with, we'll find the right doctors to get young Tiny Tim well. And we will make him well, you believe me, don't you, Bob?
Bob Cratchit (*nodding feebly*) Yes... I believe you... I believe anything.
Scrooge And may this be the merriest Christmas of all our lives!

And he is gone, covered in Children

Tiny Tim is the first to recover

Tiny Tim God bless us, every one!

Bob Cratchit opens wide his arms to embrace his wife, and with cries of infinite delight the Cratchit family joins the ever-growing, swirling Crowd and accompany Father Christmas on his merry Christmas way. Bell-ringers join in the mounting Chorus

SCENE 11

A London street—Cheapside

Company   In the mornin'—
                    Christmas morning

> If yer lift yer eyes,
> There's a big surprise!
> On yer bed you'll see
> There's a gift from Farver Chris'mas—
> From Farver Chris'mas—
> That's 'ow Chris'mas oughta be!

Scrooge and his entourage approach Tom Jenkins

Scrooge Tom Jenkins, about the six pounds you owe me!
Tom Jenkins You agreed to a few more days, Mr Scrooge—I just need——
Scrooge You can keep it! It's my Christmas present to you!

Tom Jenkins' legs give way under him

Tom Jenkins Oh! God bless you this Christmas Day, Mr Scrooge!

The music joins in as he starts to sing

> Thank you very much!!
> That's the nicest thing
> That anyone's ever done for me!

Scrooge
> It sounds a bit bizarre,
> But things the way they are,
> I feel as if another life's
> Begun for me!

And that goes for anybody else who owes me money! (*He shows them all his little black book, from which he tears out all the pages and throws them away*) You can keep it... as of this day, all my debts are forgiven!

The Crowd goes mad with delight and gives a great cheer

Tom Jenkins	An' if I'ad a drum
	I'd 'ave to bang it—
	To add a sort of rumpty-tumpty touch!
Scrooge	But since I left me drummer at 'ome,
	I'll simply 'ave ter say
Company	Thank you very, very, very much!

Scrooge ducks into the Punch and Judy tent as the music continues. Scrooge and the Punch and Judy Man duet amicably, their two smiling faces filling the tiny Punch and Judy stage. The watching audience of Children cheer and applaud

Punch	Thank you very much!
Judy	Thank you very much!
Punch and Judy Man	(*popping their heads up*) That's the nicest thing
and Scrooge	That anyone's ever done for me!
The Dilbers	It isn't every day
	Good fortune comes our way!
Scrooge	I never thought
	The future would be fun for me!

Harry and his wife enter and stare at the singing, dancing, cavorting Scrooge in total disbelief

Nephew Uncle Ebenezer? Is that you?

Scrooge Merry Christmas to you, me dear boy, and to your enchanting bride! We were just on our way to your house... with some presents. Here! These are from an old fool who deeply regrets all the Christmasses gone by that he might have shared with you! (*To Helen*) And this is for you, my dear! A sort of belated wedding gift! (*He hands the last and most elaborate package to Helen. He finds himself looking into a face hauntingly like Isabel's*)

Helen Oh, Uncle Ebenezer, thank you! Christmas lunch is sharp at three. May we expect you?

Scrooge You may! I'll be there! My word, you are a pretty girl! You remind me of... someone I used to know! (*He wipes a tear from his eye, kisses her again and smiles at his Nephew*) Now, come with us, why don't you? We're giving people presents! It's a very ... nice thing to do.

(*Singing*)	Happiness is a new friend—
	One I truly recommend.
Nephew	Happiness you will soon see
Helen and Nephew	Makes us all a family

Scrooge	(*nodding*) Now I see ...

Helen, Nephew	That happiness
and Scrooge	Is wherever love wants it to be.

The church choir, led by a Choirmaster, enters nearby, singing A Christmas Carol

Choir   Sing a song of gladness and cheer—
                             For the time of Christmas is here...

*The two groups overflow into one another, and the two songs they are singing
overlap in violent cacophony. Despite this, both keep going at full strength,
so that the unlikely duet becomes almost a competition between Scrooge and
his group and the Choirmaster and his Choirboys*

Scrooge   An' if I 'ad a cannon
  and   I would fire it—
Parade   To add a'sort of
                             Celebration touch.

                                    Choir   And enjoy the beauty—
                                                 All the joy and beauty—
                                                 That a merry Christmas
                             But since I left me   Can bring
                             Cannon at 'ome   To you!
                             I'll simply 'ave to say— Goodness and joy

                             Thank you
                             Very very   Sing a Christmas carol—
                             Very   Christmas is
                             Much!   Here!

*The Choirboys are quick to see that Scrooge's group are having much
more fun than they are. They surge forward, practically trampling the
Choirmaster underfoot in their eagerness to join Scrooge's Christmas
Parade. Suddenly the two groups become one, both imbued with the gaiety
of the Christmas spirit that is personified in Scrooge who, skipping and
dancing merrily at the head of the mob, is having more fun than he has ever
had in his life before*

All   Thank you very much!
                             Thank you very much!
                             That's the nicest thing
                             That anyone's ever done for me!
                             I may sound double-dutch,
                             But my delight is such
                             I feel as if
                             A losing war's been won for me!

                             An' if I 'ad a flag I'd 'ang me flag out
                             To add a sort of final victory touch!

But since I left me flag at 'ome

Since I left me flag at 'ome

I'll simply 'ave ter say

Simply 'ave ter
Simply 'ave ter
Say

Thank you very much!
Thank you very much!
Thank you very much!
Thank you very, very, very much!
Thank you very, very, very...

The Crowd throw their hats in the air. Church bells ring

Scrooge Merry Christmas, everyone! Merry Christmas! I have to go now and get ready... (*He starts to move off, then turns to face the audience*) I'm spending Christmas (*his voice falters for a second, but he completes the sentence proudly*) ...with my family.

No. 23a: I'll Begin Again (Reprise)

I will start anew—
I will make amends—
And I'll make quite certain
That the story ends
On a note of hope—
On a strong amen—
And I'll thank the world
And remember when
I was able to begin again!
I'll begin again!

CURTAIN

CURTAIN *calls:*

The Company is revealed up stage

No. 24: Curtain Calls

Company   Sing a song of gladness and cheer
For the time of Christmas is here!
Look around about you and see
What a world of wonder
This world can be!

The Children and Ensemble bow

Sing a Christmas carol!
Sing a Christmas carol!
Sing a Christmas carol!
Like the children do!

And enjoy the beauty—
All the joy and beauty—
That a merry Christmas
Can bring to you!

*Mr and Mrs Fezziwig; young Ebenezer and Isabel; Tom Jenkins; Marley,
the Ghost of Christmas Past, and the Ghost of Christmas Present; Bob and
Mrs Cratchit and Tiny Tim; and Scrooge enter and bow to:*

I like life!
Life likes me!
I make life a perpetual spree!
Eating food! Drinking wine!
Thinking who'd like the privilege to dine me!
I like living
The life of pleasure—
Pausing only
To take my leisure!

I like songs! I like dance!
I hear music and I'm in a trance.
Tra-la-la! Oom-pa-pah!
Chances are
I shall get up and prance.
Where there's music and laughter,
Happiness is rife!

Scrooge   Why?
Company   Because I like life!

The Company bow

They present the orchestra

The Company bow

Scrooge, Ghosts of Christmas Past and Present, and Marley step forward

Scrooge steps forward

The Company all join hands and sing

No. 24a: Thank You Very Much (Reprise)

Company   Thank you very, very, very much!
                     Thank you very, very, very much!

The Company exit to the wings

Scrooge, The Ghost of Christmas Present and Marley link arms and exit upstage, dancing

No. 25: Playout

THE END

Chestnuts
Twelfth-cakes
Bowls of punch with dry ice
White fluid
2 huge chalices

SCENE 12

On stage: A LONDON STREET—CHEAPSIDE
Harry and **Helen's** gifts
Glasses for **Tom Jenkins** and **Beggar Woman**

ACT II

SCENE 1

On stage: A LONDON STREET—CHEAPSIDE

Set: THE CRATCHITS' HOUSE
Copper containing small, muslin-wrapped plum pudding
Copper-stick
Punchbowl with tiny glasses
Wine
Eggcups
Wooden spoon
Crockery platter with small, poorly plucked goose
Stuffing

SCENE 2

On stage: THE CRATCHITS' HOUSE:
As at end of previous scene

stage: Copper coins (**Tiny Tim**)

SCENE 3

tage: SCROOGE'S NEPHEW'S SITTING-ROOM
Sofa
Coffee-table
Lit candles. Drinks
Bottle of port

FURNITURE AND PROPERTY LIST

Further dressing may be added at the director's discretion

ACT I

SCENE 1

On stage: A LONDON STREET—CHEAPSIDE
Tumbling profusion of Christmas fare

SCENE 2

On stage: SCROOGE'S OFFICE
Clerk's tall desk and chair. *On desk:* paper, pen, ink
Candle (burned down)
Scrooge's desk and chair. *On desk:* ledger
Gold coins
Money box
Safe
Large leather-bound ledgers
Dusty bookcase with locking doors
Fireplace with one lump of coal
Coal scuttle

Personal: **Scrooge**: walking stick, watch-chain with keys, pocket watch, purse
with money; ring on chain round neck (worn throughout)
Nephew: fob watch

SCENE 3

On stage: A LONDON STREET—CHEAPSIDE
Stalls and shops containing various wares and food including:
Toy shop with model carousel and decorated Christmas tree, doll etc.
Bakery stall with small parcel
Fruit stall laden with fruit
Wine store with bottles, carpet bag, stone jar
Butcher's shop with enormous turkey, scraggy goose

Knitwear stall
Punch and Judy tent with puppets
Soup trolley with can of broth

Off stage: Beautifully wrapped parcels (**Shoppers**)
Baby, begging bowl (**Beggar Woman**)
Giant turkey (**Bissett**)

Personal: **Bob Cratchit:** money
Scrooge: black book, pen, walking stick, keys

SCENE 4

No props required

SCENE 5

On stage: SCROOGE'S HALLWAY
Table. *On it:* candle in candle-holder, matches

SCENE 6

On stage: SCROOGE'S BEDROOM
Bed
Bedside table. *On it*: alarm clock
Straightbacked chair. Table. *On it*: spoon, bowl
Old wing-backed armchair
Fireplace. *In it*: hob, cash box. *Beside it*: poker, bell
Cupboard
Nightgown
Pom-pommed nightcap
Bedsocks
Slippers
Full length mirror

Personal: **Marley**: great chain of cash-boxes, ledgers, keys, padlocks, deeds,
heavy purses

SCENE 7

On stage: A SCHOOL-ROOM
Row of school benches and chairs

Furniture and Property List

Pile of labelled suitcases
Boy Ebenezer's possessions

SCENE 8

On stage: FEZZIWIG'S WAREHOUSE
Warehouse signs

Off stage: Tall desk with bell (**Two Young Men**)
Balloons, ribbons (**Party Guests**)
Food, drink, packages (**Bakery Girls and Winery Boys**)
Multi-tiered Christmas cake (**Isabel**)
Fiddle (**Fiddler**)

Personal: **Fezziwig**: fob watch
Ebenezer: ring

SCENE 9

On stage: EBENEZER'S OFFICE
Desk. *On it*: papers, pen, vase of faded flowers, money box ,
gold coins, pair of scales
Chair

Off stage: Bunch of flowers (**Isabel**)

Personal: **Isabel**: ring

SCENE 10

On stage: SCROOGE'S BEDROOM
As for Scene 6

SCENE 11

Set: SCROOGE'S BEDROOM
Holly
Mistletoe
Ivy
Joints of meat, game and poultry
Suckling pigs
Mince-pies
Plum puddings
Barrels of oysters

Off stage: Large basket of presents **(Helen)**

Personal: **Christmas Present:** silver goblet, 2 glasses, oversized leg of turkey
                 Topper: blindfold

SCENE 4

On stage: SCROOGE'S BEDROOM
                 As for ACT I, SCENE 6

SCENE 5

On stage: THE STREET OUTSIDE SCROOGE'S OFFICE
                 Handcart

Off stage: **Scrooge's** black book **(Tom Jenkins)**
                 Coffin **(Men)**
                 Scrooge's possessions **(Dilbers)**

SCENE 6

On stage: THE CRATCHITS' HOUSE
                 Table
                 Chairs
                 Sewing
                 Book

SCENE 7

On stage: THE CHURCHYARD
                 Tiny Tim's grave with simple white wooden cross
                 Bunch of violets
                 Scrooge's grave with large, grey, flat slab

Off stage: Immense chain **(Four Figures)**

SCENE 8

On stage: SCROOGE'S BEDROOM
                 As for ACT I, SCENE 6

SCENE 9

On stage: A LONDON STREET—CHEAPSIDE
              Snow
              Toys in shop window
              Case of wine in wine merchant's

Off stage: Gigantic turkey **(Boy)**
              Gift-wrapped packages **(Mr Pringle** and **Assistants)**
              Handcarts **(Urchins)**
              Santa sack **(Scrooge)**
              Sled **(Urchins)**

Personal: **Pringle:** pad, pen
              Scrooge: money

SCENE 10

On stage: THE CRATCHITS' HOUSE

Off stage: 2 leather purses containing coins **(Scrooge)**
              Wrapped presents, including one containing toy carousel and one
              containing doll **(Children)**

SCENE 11

On stage: A LONDON STREET—CHEAPSIDE
              Punch and Judy tent

Personal: **Scrooge:** black book

LIGHTING PLOT

Property fittings required: nil. Practical fittings required: 'miserable fire' in Scrooge's bedroom
Interior and exterior settings

ACT I, Scene 1

To open: London street, winter evening
No cues

ACT I, Scene 2

To open: Cross-fade to **Scrooge's** office

No cues

ACT I, Scene 3

To open: Cross-fade to London street, winter evening
No cues

ACT I, Scene 4

To open:	Cross-fade to **Scrooge's** front door	
Cue 1	**Scrooge** looks at door knocker	(Page 17)
	Cold white spot on door knocker for ghastly effect	
Cue 2	**Marley's face**: "Scroo-o-o-o-ge!"	(Page 17)
	Fade spot	

ACT I, SCENE 5

To open: Cross-fade to **Scrooge's** hallway, gloomy evening

Cue 3	**Scrooge** lights candle	(Page 17)
	Flickering flame and shadow effect	

ACT I, SCENE 6

To open: Cross-fade to **Scrooge's** bedroom, gloomy evening, "miserable fire" effect

Cue 4	**Marley** throws a loop of his chain over **Scrooge**	(Page 20)
	Strange lights shine through windows and doors	

Cue 5	**Scrooge**: "No, Jacob! No-o-o-o!"	(Page 20)
	Ghastly effect on **Phantoms**	

Cue 6	**Marley**: "Is far, far worse!"	(Page 22)
	Fade lights on **Phantoms,** *reverting to gloomy interior*	

Cue 7	**Scrooge** lights candle	(Page 23)
	Flickering flame and shadow effect	

Cue 8	**Scrooge:** "...and nothing else?"	(Page 24)
	Blinding light	

ACT I, SCENE 7

To open: Cross-fade to school-room interior

No cues

ACT I, SCENE 8

To open: Cross-fade to Fezziwig's bright warehouse interior

No cues

92 Scrooge—The Musical

Cue 14 **Scrooge** touches **Christmas Present's** robe (Page 47)
Blinding flash of light

ACT II, Scene 2

To open: Full interior lighting in **Cratchits'** house

Cue 15 **Scrooge** touches **Christmas Present's** robe (Page 52)
Blinding flash of light

ACT II, Scene 3

To open: Firelight and candle glow in **Nephew's** sitting-room

No cues

ACT II, Scene 4

To open: Cross-fade to Scrooge's gloomy bedroom; "miserable fire" effect

Cue 16 **Phantom** raises both arms (Page 61)
Lightning

ACT II, Scene 5

To open: Cross-fade to daylight on street

No cues

ACT II, Scene 6

To open: Cross-fade to **Cratchit's** house

No cues

ACT II, Scene 7

To open: Cross-fade to bleak, grey churchyard

ACT I, Scene 9

To open: Cross-fade to **Ebenezer's** office

No cues

ACT I, Scene 10

To open: Cross-fade to **Scrooge's** gloomy bedroom; "miserable fire" effect

No cues

ACT I, Scene 11

To open: Deepen gloom in **Scrooge's** bedroom

Cue 9	Church bell strikes two o'clock *Bring up strange glow of light*	(Page 39)
Cue 10	**Scrooge**: "There's nothing to be afraid of!" *Brighten glow*	(Page 39)
Cue 11	**Christmas Present** *(off)*: "No, it's not!" *Intensify glow*	(Page 39)
Cue 12	Feast is revealed *Soften light*	(Page 39)

ACT I, Scene 12

To open: Cross-fade to London street, winter evening

No cues

ACT II, Scene 1

To open: London street, winter night

Cue 13	**Christmas Present** snaps his fingers *Reveal* **Cratchits'** *kitchen parlour*	(Page 47)

FURNITURE AND PROPERTY LIST

Further dressing may be added at the director's discretion

ACT I

Scene 1

On stage: A London Street—Cheapside
Tumbling profusion of Christmas fare

Scene 2

On stage: Scrooge's office
Clerk's tall desk and chair. *On desk:* paper, pen, ink
Candle (burned down)
Scrooge's desk and chair. *On desk:* ledger
Gold coins
Money box
Safe
Large leather-bound ledgers
Dusty bookcase with locking doors
Fireplace with one lump of coal
Coal scuttle

Personal: **Scrooge**: walking stick, watch-chain with keys, pocket watch, purse
with money; ring on chain round neck (worn throughout)
Nephew: fob watch

Scene 3

On stage: A London Street—Cheapside
Stalls and shops containing various wares and food including:
Toy shop with model carousel and decorated Christmas tree, doll etc.
Bakery stall with small parcel
Fruit stall laden with fruit
Wine store with bottles, carpet bag, stone jar
Butcher's shop with enormous turkey, scraggy goose

          Knitwear stall
          Punch and Judy tent with puppets
          Soup trolley with can of broth

Off stage: Beautifully wrapped parcels **(Shoppers)**
          Baby, begging bowl **(Beggar Woman)**
          Giant turkey **(Bissett)**

Personal: **Bob Cratchit:** money
          Scrooge: black book, pen, walking stick, keys

Scene 4

No props required

Scene 5

On stage: SCROOGE'S HALLWAY
          Table. *On it:* candle in candle-holder, matches

Scene 6

On stage: SCROOGE'S BEDROOM
          Bed
          Bedside table. *On it*: alarm clock
          Straightbacked chair. Table. *On it*: spoon, bowl
          Old wing-backed armchair
          Fireplace. *In it*: hob, cash box. *Beside it*: poker, bell
          Cupboard
          Nightgown
          Pom-pommed nightcap
          Bedsocks
          Slippers
          Full length mirror

Personal: **Marley**: great chain of cash-boxes, ledgers, keys, padlocks, deeds,
          heavy purses

Scene 7

On stage: A SCHOOL-ROOM
          Row of school benches and chairs

Pile of labelled suitcases
Boy Ebenezer's possessions

SCENE 8

On stage: FEZZIWIG'S WAREHOUSE
Warehouse signs

Off stage: Tall desk with bell **(Two Young Men)**
Balloons, ribbons **(Party Guests)**
Food, drink, packages **(Bakery Girls and Winery Boys)**
Multi-tiered Christmas cake **(Isabel)**
Fiddle **(Fiddler)**

Personal: **Fezziwig**: fob watch
Ebenezer: ring

SCENE 9

On stage: EBENEZER'S OFFICE
Desk. *On it:* papers, pen, vase of faded flowers, money box with
gold coins, pair of scales
Chair

Off stage: Bunch of flowers **(Isabel)**

Personal: **Isabel:** ring

SCENE 10

On stage: SCROOGE'S BEDROOM
As for Scene 6

SCENE 11

Set: SCROOGE'S BEDROOM
Holly
Mistletoe
Ivy
Joints of meat, game and poultry
Suckling pigs
Mince-pies
Plum puddings
Barrels of oysters

Chestnuts
Twelfth-cakes
Bowls of punch with dry ice
White fluid
2 huge chalices

Scene 12

On stage: A London street—Cheapside
               Harry and **Helen's** gifts
               Glasses for **Tom Jenkins** and **Beggar Woman**

ACT II

Scene 1

On stage: A London street—Cheapside

Set: The Cratchits' house
               Copper containing small, muslin-wrapped plum pudding
               Copper-stick
               Punchbowl with tiny glasses
               Wine
               Eggcups
               Wooden spoon
               Crockery platter with small, poorly plucked goose
               Stuffing

Scene 2

On stage: The Cratchits' house:
               As at end of previous scene

Off stage: Copper coins (**Tiny Tim**)

Scene 3

On stage: Scrooge's Nephew's sitting-room
               Sofa
               Coffee-table
               Lit candles. Drinks
               Bottle of port

ACT I, Scene 5

To open: Cross-fade to **Scrooge's** hallway, gloomy evening

| *Cue* 3 | **Scrooge** lights candle | (Page 17) |
| | *Flickering flame and shadow effect* | |

ACT I, Scene 6

To open: Cross-fade to **Scrooge's** bedroom, gloomy evening, "miserable fire" effect

| *Cue* 4 | **Marley** throws a loop of his chain over **Scrooge** | (Page 20) |
| | *Strange lights shine through windows and doors* | |

| *Cue* 5 | **Scrooge**: "No, Jacob! No-o-o-o!" | (Page 20) |
| | *Ghastly effect on* **Phantoms** | |

| *Cue* 6 | **Marley**: "Is far, far worse!" | (Page 22) |
| | *Fade lights on* **Phantoms,** *reverting to gloomy interior* | |

| *Cue* 7 | **Scrooge** lights candle | (Page 23) |
| | *Flickering flame and shadow effect* | |

| *Cue* 8 | **Scrooge:** "...and nothing else?" | (Page 24) |
| | *Blinding light* | |

ACT I, Scene 7

To open: Cross-fade to school-room interior

No cues

ACT I, Scene 8

To open: Cross-fade to Fezziwig's bright warehouse interior

No cues

LIGHTING PLOT

Property fittings required: nil. Practical fittings required: 'miserable fire' in Scrooge's bedroom
Interior and exterior settings

ACT I, Scene 1

To open: London street, winter evening
No cues

ACT I, Scene 2

To open: Cross-fade to **Scrooge's** office

No cues

ACT I, Scene 3

To open: Cross-fade to London street, winter evening
No cues

ACT I, Scene 4

To open:	Cross-fade to **Scrooge's** front door	
Cue 1	**Scrooge** looks at door knocker	(Page 17)
	Cold white spot on door knocker for ghastly effect	
Cue 2	**Marley's face**: "Scroo-o-o-o-ge!"	(Page 17)
	Fade spot	

SCENE 9

On stage: A LONDON STREET—CHEAPSIDE
               Snow
               Toys in shop window
               Case of wine in wine merchant's

Off stage: Gigantic turkey **(Boy)**
               Gift-wrapped packages **(Mr Pringle** and **Assistants)**
               Handcarts **(Urchins)**
               Santa sack **(Scrooge)**
               Sled **(Urchins)**

Personal: **Pringle:** pad, pen
               Scrooge: money

SCENE 10

On stage: THE CRATCHITS' HOUSE

Off stage: 2 leather purses containing coins **(Scrooge)**
               Wrapped presents, including one containing toy carousel and one
               containing doll **(Children)**

SCENE 11

On stage: A LONDON STREET—CHEAPSIDE
               Punch and Judy tent

Personal: **Scrooge:** black book

Off stage: Large basket of presents **(Helen)**

Personal: **Christmas Present:** silver goblet, 2 glasses, oversized leg of turkey
                Topper: blindfold

SCENE 4

On stage: SCROOGE'S BEDROOM
                As for ACT I, SCENE 6

SCENE 5

On stage: THE STREET OUTSIDE SCROOGE'S OFFICE
                Handcart

Off stage: **Scrooge's** black book **(Tom Jenkins)**
                Coffin **(Men)**
                Scrooge's possessions **(Dilbers)**

SCENE 6

On stage: THE CRATCHITS' HOUSE
                Table
                Chairs
                Sewing
                Book

SCENE 7

On stage: THE CHURCHYARD
                Tiny Tim's grave with simple white wooden cross
                Bunch of violets
                Scrooge's grave with large, grey, flat slab

Off stage: Immense chain **(Four Figures)**

SCENE 8

On stage: SCROOGE'S BEDROOM
                As for ACT I, SCENE 6

Cue 17	**Phantom** points to Scrooge's grave	(Page 67)
	Spot on **Scrooge's** *gravestone*	

Cue 18	**Phantom** vanishes	(Page 68)
	Darken lights on **Scrooge**	

ACT II, SCENE 8

To open: Cross-fade to **Scrooge's** gloomy bedroom

Cue 19	**Scrooge** throws back the curtains	(Page 69)
	Bright daylight flooding into room	

Cue 20	Scrooge's bedroom dissolves	(Page 69)
	Bright daylight in street	

Cue 21	**Scrooge**: "Of that mountain I must climb!"	(Page 70)
	Spot on mirror, revealing faces of **Ghosts**	

ACT II, SCENE 9

To open: Cross-fade to morning in London street

No cues

ACT II, SCENE 10

To open: Cross-fade to **Cratchits'** house

No cues

ACT II, SCENE 11

To open: Cross-fade to daylight in London street

No cues

EFFECTS PLOT

ACT I

Cue 1   To open SCENE 1   (Page 1)
              Church bells chime six o 'clock

Cue 2   **Bob Cratchit** warms his hands on candle   (Page 5)
              Church bells chime seven o 'clock

Cue 3   **Scrooge**: "...this very night."   (Page 14)
              Ominous rumble of thunder

Cue 4   **Scrooge:** "Humbug!"   (Page 16)
              Great crack of thunder

Cue 5   **Scrooge** lights candle   (Page 17)
              Wind effect strengthening

Cue 6   **Scrooge** runs for his sitting-room   (Page 17)
              *Echoes of running footsteps, augmenting and multiplying
              in sound, then slowly fading away*

Cue 7   **Scrooge** places the soup-can on the hob   (Page 18)
              Wind moans mournfully

Cue 8   **Scrooge** slops gruel back into the bowl   (Page 18)
              Wind moans mournfully, echoing **Scrooge's** *name,
              smoke billows from chimney*

Cue 9   Bell starts to swing   (Page 18)
              Sound of bells increasing, echoing, then silence

Cue 10   **Scrooge** uncovers his ears and listens intently   (Page 18)
              *Deep hollow clanking sound and heavy footsteps outside
              his door*

Cue 11   **Scrooge** puts his ear to the door   (Page 18)
              *Reverberating echoes of dragging chains, creaking
              doors, dismal wailing and muffled footsteps*

Cue 12   **Scrooge** puts the cash box under his pillow   (Page 18)
            Bolts slide back and key turns, unlocking door

Cue 13   **Scrooge** hurries to the door   (Page 18)
            Increasing sound of rushing, howling wind shaking door;
            *   door flies open; great rush of icy air blows across room*

Cue 14   **Marley:** (*wailing*) Ebenezer Scroo-o-ooge!"   (Page 19)
            Door slams shut

Cue 15   **Marley** sits   (Page 19)
            Clanking of chains

Cue 16   **Marley** makes a hand gesture   (Page 20)
            Door closes

Cue 17   **Marley** shakes his chain   (Page 20)
            Clanking of chains

Cue 18   **Marley** throws chain over **Scrooge**   (Page 20)
            Doors and windows slowly open
            *   Dry ice for mist comes through*

Cue 19   The **Phantoms** fade   (Page 22)
            Doors and windows close

Cue 20   **Marley**: "...learn from them."   (Page 22)
            Midnight strikes in distance

Cue 21   **Scrooge** draws the bed curtains closed   (Page 24)
            Church clock strikes full chimes of one o'clock with deep
            *   melancholy boom*

Cue 22   **Children** exit   (Page 26)
            Children's *voices echo and fade away*

Cue 23   **Scrooge**: "No, it's not—my..."   (Page 39)
            Church bell strikes two o'clock

ACT II

Cue 24   **Scrooge**: "And learn to live it well!"   (Page 60)
            Church bells chime three o'clock in distance; macabre
            *   and ghostly sounds*

Cue 25	**Phantom** raises both arms	(Page 61)
	Thunder; howling, icy gale blows through room, increasing to typhoon	
Cue 26	**Marley** appears	(Page 68)
	Clanking of chains	
Cue 27	**Four figures** appear	(Page 68)
	Heavy clanking effects	
Cue 28	**Scrooge** clutches desperately at **Ghost**	(Page 68)
	Spine-chilling banshee wail	
Cue 29	The lights darken on **Scrooge**	(Page 68)
	Echoing, receding cries from **Scrooge**	
Cue 30	**Scrooge** laughs and cries with joy	(Page 70)
	Church bells chime nine o 'clock	
Cue 31	**The Crowd** throw their hats in the air	(Page 80)
	Church bells ring	